PENGUIN BOOKS
HOW TO RIDE A TRAIN TO
ULAANBAATAR AND OTHER ESSAYS

Josephine V. Roque writes essays, profiles, reviews, short stories, and plays. She has worked and contributed to print and online publications in Manila and overseas. Joyce graduated with an MFA in Creative Writing from De La Salle University and received prizes from the Palanca Awards, Doreen Fernandez Food Writing Awards and the Ateneo Art Awards. She is currently working on a new collection of short stories.

# How to Ride a Train to Ulaanbaatar and Other Essays

Josephine V. Roque

**PENGUIN BOOKS**

An imprint of Penguin Random House

PENGUIN BOOKS

USA | Canada | UK | Ireland | Australia
New Zealand | India | South Africa | China | Southeast Asia

Penguin Books is part of the Penguin Random House group of companies
whose addresses can be found at global.penguinrandomhouse.com

Published by Penguin Random House SEA Pte Ltd
9, Changi South Street 3, Level 08-01,
Singapore 486361

Penguin
Random House
SEA

First published in Penguin Books by Penguin Random House SEA 2021

Copyright © Josephine V. Roque 2021

This is my account of living in Shanghai, China, from 2007 to 2010,
and returning in 2013. I based the essays from what I remembered of that
time as well as notebook entries, conversations with friends, documents and
photos. Names and other identifying details were changed in the process of
making sense of the truth in these events.

ISBN 9789814882880

Typeset in Adobe Caslon Pro by Manipal Technologies Limited, Manipal

www.penguin.sg

*To my mother*

# Contents

# HONG KONG

# MACAU

# ULAANBAATAR

# SHANGHAI

# Upriver

In remembered memory, the Huangpu River was a glassy layer of calm reflecting jewel-toned neon lights and smelling of rusted brown pipes. Sedimented and metallic-scented water came gushing out of the shower like a baptism by yellow river during my first week in Shanghai. Was this the poo in Huangpu? Likely plain chlorinated water going through the tubes of the building where I was staying. I couldn't help but wonder about the river separating downtown Puxi, where I lived, with suburban Pudong. Stand on the Puxi side, across you saw a disco-balled future where buildings looked like gleaming bottle-openers and twinkling jackstones were not children's toys but part of the landscape. Other cities dreamed of what lay ahead, in Shanghai, it had already arrived. The Pudong side was storied, romanticized in art deco, and jazz built on the dreams of Jewish merchants plying the opium trade. The Huangpu was a man-made river, a way to control nature that threatened to inundate a city with flood, though now the same waterway could be seen in a double exposure with two images of a place for a unifying one.

I arrived on the heels of a closing winter and the beginning of a calendar: The Year of the Golden Pig. The twelfth sign of the zodiac and the last to arrive after the emperor's call according to legend. The pig's natural element is water, but that time, Shanghai was frigid and empty of people, its moving chi. A million-numbered crowd made the long journey back to the places of their childhood for New Year, like salmon using all their energy in the search for their home stream. There I was a foreigner arriving, far away from where I was born. Those who could leave, pitied those who were left behind because they could not join the festival. I unpacked bags at the Number 2 International Student Residence Hall at East China Normal University, wondering which hall was Number 1, and was there a Number 3? Why then was I assigned to a second placer? The language made it easier to assign numbers, not names. A figure was unique, monosyllabic like a chant carrying fewer chances for mispronunciation or misunderstanding. Numbers were understood in relation to the words they sounded similar to. The number four was avoided because it sounded too much like the word for death. Even words in English were not exempted and is the same reason why colleagues would admonish me for using the term, deadline, in emails which sounded to them like a death-line. Names and numbers were prized for their auspiciousness in attracting happiness or money luck like a magnet.

In a country of a billion people multiplied by billions of choices for things that dictate a life, a number was clear comprehension. Rankings made decisions more straightforward. It was a constraint that encouraged one to follow the crowd and want what everybody else wanted instead of choosing based on idiosyncratic instincts. Would you go somewhere that wasn't ranked and vetted by others? There is a harmony of tastes fitted for the majority to want, see and feel the same things. I went contrary to where other Filipinos would go, which was the top two schools in Shanghai, Fudan and Jiaoda. Huadong Shifan Daxue or Huashida, as locals liked to call it, was considered part of the top five schools in the city, a legacy of the Anglicans since 1879. A stranger led me here based on advice given in a chat room, then over email. There would be fewer English speakers there, he said. More vitally, the tuition would be cheaper, a grave concern for someone self-financed like me. It was a dream of mine to work in another country and learn a foreign language. Huashida was called a garden university because of its weeping willow trees leaning towards a ribbon of the river as if listening for gurgles. It was a classic scene that would repeat itself in varying measures of serenity as I travelled around the country.

I shared a room with Noodles, a Japanese woman in her late twenties, during her first year in China. It was a name I called her in my head after I accidentally spilled her bowl of ramen on the floor, something she would never forgive me for. She would not say it but no translation was needed to know she was upset. So the third roommate between us was called Silence because Noodles and I barely understood each other. She spoke no English, and I mumbled the words I knew over and over in Mandarin: I, yes, no, maybe, very bad, I don't know and please. I was reduced to a blubbering mess. She asked me if I did not mind if she prayed. Noodles prayed like clockwork, kneeling on the bed in the afternoons, then stretching her arms, up, up, high up while chanting as she ended the session with palms on the chest and head bowed. A kraft envelope arrived from Japan, weekly, that I would sometimes hand the package to her and watch her read it. Noodles was part of a religious group that worshiped nature and believed heaven was a place on top of a sacred mountain, cloudy and serene. Why not? I met a Laotian from the same hall who told me he believed in animals and asked perplexed — were all women in the Philippines free to be on her own like me? What did I know about religious groups in Japan?

Nothing but what the news told me about an attack on Japanese subways. Inside our room, I would look out the window, the trees in the half-light, an oval running track with people walking backward like tape looping in reverse and wondered if I could ask her about non-believers such as myself, did we deserve an afterlife? What was the Mandarin word for a cult without risking offense? Quiet answered the question for me. Noodles spoke to me as if from a pulpit, careful to pronounce the tones slowly so I could catch it like a child catching butterflies with their bare hands. I love China; I want very much to marry a Chinese man, she told me in Mandarin. I answered in mangled tones that made her face wince. Brutal sounds assaulted her ears. I could not blame her. Listening was language, and if she listened to my pronunciation, I would drag her down with me, and both of us would not be any wiser.

After Noodles, Glitter came next, a 17-year-old Vietnamese who liked shiny things. She believed in Hello Kitty and Vietnam, introducing herself as a proud citizen from the country that beat America. Touché. I came from the country that was duped by America, I thought, the land sold by Spain behind our back. Glitter's father was a general in the army. She was a vision in pink and sequins. They lived one hour from Hanoi, where winter weather from China dropped the temperature enough to to allow people to dream of winter. Vietnamese was a tonal language with borrowed words from Mandarin, a legacy of the time they were a Chinese colony for 1,000 years. Glitter went from barely saying *ni hao* to almost fluent in a matter of weeks. The same pattern surfaced. Again we would not understand each other as she grew impatient with my language aptitude because I was falling behind. She introduced me to the other Vietnamese students in the residence on teaching scholarship from China.

I would write down her recipe for pork spring rolls, the meat ground by hand, and sprinkled with crushed bouillon cubes. I watched her cook it in a room where I almost burned a friend's stove. She had the domestic skills of someone twice her age as she hand-washed clothes every day. I looked down on my hands, red from trying to wash denim, and bought laundry tokens instead.

Glitter was curious about why I remained unmarried while of marriageable age. No one will want you when you are older, she said. She had a whole life planned out for her: studies in China, a job in Vietnam, then marriage and kids. I knew she received her allowance by the number of Hello Kitties that would multiply around me. From a clock, the cat that was not a cat, crawled on to invade the rest of the room to dresses, laptops, pens, bags, shoes, and finally, one bigger than a human head tacked on the refrigerator door.

As for me, I believed in English. I relied on it to save me from the unknowable and foreign as it did when I spoke to blond, blue-eyed playmates while growing up in Angeles City, Pampanga. To be understood was to speak in English, and the world's tragedies were explained to me in English in newspapers, television, movies, and books. Tagalog and Kapampangan came with stories in comic books and talk during meals. Our neighbours were families escaping the confines of Clark Air Base, who liked staying outside for the cheaper rents and beyond the reach of base rules. Those days passed with fiestas mixed with American holidays: imported candies for Halloween, turkey holidays for Thanksgiving, and pine cones for Christmas. In between were black market PX goods in Dau or wishing for ice cream in a paper carton. My mother bought me an American schoolhouse table, laminated white with metal legs and black rubber feet, where I sat to read fairy tales and scribbled paper with crayons. There were freshly baked tollhouse cookies from a Filipino who married a Texan. I knew not all women were like her — lucky.

Another neighbour woke up to the sounds of screaming and slapping in the mornings from her husband. The Americans were gone for good in 1991 when the airbase channel turned static black, and I could no longer watch cartoons. The large, white American stove in our kitchen was one of the spoils of their hasty retreat. It was the one thing my father was able to get in the gold rush that ensued as people seized cars, furniture and other valuables left by the fleeing military. In the end, it was not the protests that would drive them away or the votes of a jaded senate disgusted by American complicity to Marcos rule, but an angry volcano. Mount Pinatubo, in a fit, had done what Filipinos have been trying to do for hundreds of years: Kick the foreigners out. They left, but their ghosts stayed, minds and hearts still colonized. English shaped what I knew of the world as much as Tagalog or Kapampangan did.

I realized the mistake of this belief on the first day on campus. No one spoke English. Not on the line to register for classes, in the canteen or at the dormitories. The lingua franca of the international students was either French or Korean. I was mute and stupid, not to be able to express the simplest of ideas. Some of them would find the misuse of words hilarious when I would switch male and female names in Mandarin. A *jiangshi* ghost dressed in a Qing dynasty garb would hop away from me if he heard me talk. *Dui bu qi, ting bu dong*, I would apologize. Learning a new language was replete with the hazards of public humiliation. Westerners presumed since I was Asian that somehow the Chinese language was related to

ours the way the Romance languages were to each other.
No. I would meet people from former French colonies
in the country on language scholarships. The year was
2007, and China was pouring money into Africa, unafraid
to deal with despots shunned by the West but eager to
mine it for the metals it needed to continue growing
like an expanding balloon not yet finding shape. The
most popular guy on campus was a friendly Mauritian
who spoke English, French and Spanish in China on
self-imposed exile by his father, who told him never to go
back. It was at his birthday party that I would meet the
winners of Ms Africa in Shanghai, who were sculptural,
tall and leggy in their alabaster beauty.

I questioned why I was there in the first place when
I was lazy and horrible with languages. I barely spoke
Spanish despite studying it since high school, and my
Kapampangan fluency was limited to listening to family
gossip. It would be years later that I would understand why:
because back then it was the zeitgeist, an Asian country
poised to become the largest economy in the world. It was
also because of the people I knew. Friends had gone after
graduation. I grew up with an uncle who went to China
after it opened up in 1979, criss-crossing the country in
trains, with a Communist. He brought home watercolour
landscape paintings from his adventures and stories. But
most of all, I was there because my mother died. She was
the only one who could have stopped me from leaving.
I surprised myself at how my voice sounded like talking in
Mandarin, in a sing-song, careful not to say the wrong tone

both metaphorically and literally. Talking in another language, I became a different person. When I did hear someone speak in English, it would be Claws and Dax, who were Canadian and British respectively. I would latch on to them like a life vest. Finally, relieved. I mastered the first phrases I would speak with confidence and say again and again:

*Wo shi Feilubin ren.*
*Wo shi Feilubin ren.*
*Wo shi Feilubin ren.*
*Shi, Wo Feilubin ren.*
*Wo Feilubin ren.*
*Wo Feilubin.*
*Wo ren.*
*Wo*
I am Filipino.
I am Filipino.
*Ako ay Pilipino.*
*Ako ay Pilipino.*
*Ako ay Pilipino.*

These words, I said out loud so many times, it became a mantra. It was the answer to a question asked even before your name. I learned more about being Filipino by being outside the country than in it, where I never had to answer for people I belonged with, but never knew personally. Back home, I did not think of those who I passed by on the street or encountered in public places because they were like me: dealing with a monsoon that flipped umbrellas inside out, flooded roads and bore down on leaky rooftops; or in the summer, the baking heat that made the brow sticky wet after a shower, and for respite to the chilly shopping malls turned into informal public spaces of sorts where you could skate on ice while it was 36 degrees Celsius outside or dealing with oppressive traffic that made moving from one point to another a practice in existential absurdity. It was a pendulum that swung from keeping abreast with the news cycle and ignoring it for sanity maintenance because if you paid too much attention and felt every headline, you might stop breathing at the infuriating madness of it all. Yet, when I lived in China, there was a vacuum. Information was like listening to the slow heartbeat of a tortoise. I did not know what was happening in Shanghai, much less the rest of the country or the world. There was gossip repeated and passed on during lunch breaks or subway commute. Colleagues would tell me what they heard over radio. The newspaper was scant, boring as if asking you to move along and to read other things. One had to go through a proxy server to get reliable information about home. There was a deafening silence where there used to be a polyphony of voices fighting to get attention.

*

I moved out of the student residences reluctantly after finding a job working for an English publishing company, a search that did not happen fast because I knew no one, and outside the country, a diploma from a prestigious local university meant nothing. I was anxious to find a place of my own because of the higher expense and risk of living with people I did not know. At the dorms, I made friends, the staff knew me. There was a park. I knew where to buy food when hungry. The apartment search ended up with two other Filipinos who were friends of friends of friends, this system of understanding people, *mga kakilala*, that unearths even the forgotten details of your past like who you rode a school bus with while in kindergarten to build on tenuous connections at best. Exp was like me, not Chinese, not a *huayi*, having gone to China on scholarship. A former competitive swimmer, she learned Mandarin with the doggedness of an athlete and worked as a shift manager at one of the most popular restaurants in town. She was the second-most fluent speaker I knew who could tell you a movie plot without pause in Mandarin. My other flatmate was Tea, who worked as an architect for a British firm since graduation from Manila. I took the smallest room in the flat, beside the cramped living room stuffed with Tea's sketched studies of interiors and buildings, including a hotel in Hangzhou where she was interviewed on Chinese radio about design. Living with them did not improve my Mandarin and was hampered by the fact that they were much better speakers. I got discouraged and timid talking in front of them. Tea would volunteer to translate brochures for me. Exp would hold out her arm and say she would haggle rent with the landlord.

All of them would pale in comparison to Ahya, who was the best. More than a decade in the mainland, his mother was Filipino, while his father was a second-generation Chinese immigrant. He looked Malay but grew up reading Chinese comic books. I met him of all places while lining up for dinner, where a friend and I were talking in Tagalog. Ahya worked in the business of due diligence or digging of secrets as I liked teasing him. His boss was a former British agent who opened a consultancy firm in the mainland for foreign clients dealing with Chinese partners. Their job was to fish for things people lied about: debts, addictions, mistresses and other fictions. Ahya could read financial reports and contracts in Mandarin. So well-known was he for this that we would take our documents to him to make sure we were not being duped. He would negotiate for companies to do work in China. I did not ask how he knew so much about me when I knew but the bare facts about him. He became a friend who talked about many things other than himself, as I would tell these stories, not mine, of people who only continue to exist in memories of place. What I did know for sure was that he liked music, and during our weekend afternoon walks along the French Concession, we would stop to eavesdrop on musicians practising the scales and etudes of Tchaikovsky and Chopin at the Shanghai Music Academy. The music flowed and ebbed like seawater on an immeasurable shoreline. We stood outside and imagined the musician's heads bent at an angle, the pressure of performing gone, their face relaxed for the pleasure of playing music, and for the intended audience. I remembered his blue check coat, and it would be that sleeve I would follow as he dragged me to jazz bars in the city, and once while we watched a band play, squeezed into a corner and woozy from Cuba libres, he told me to come nearer. I leaned in thinking he might want to steal a kiss but instead was told a story: Of getting the fingerprints of Kim Jong-Il in North Korea; a tall tale.

Aren't you afraid?
The trick is not to do it yourself.

They hired Chinese sleuths to do the work for them. The other trick was to stop asking questions. Lest you get disappointed in a jazz bar, again. There was no way of confirming if what he said was true; if the office I had visited him in with people hunched over narrow tables, staring at laptops did what they said they did. Trust was a test I always took. Another person would tell me while waiting for a cab on a spring day that her father had been a spy, a double agent for the Americans. I commented about double espresso shot coffees, pretending to have misheard. She answered that maybe she had read too much Eileen Chang and Agnes Smedley. I routinely heard exaggerations. A British man who looked like Richard Branson, would tell me he was a duke with a castle. The claim was correct, but the title was not through birth right, a hard-up royal had sold it on the internet. A Filipino would say, not knowing I was in the group, that he graduated from the best university in the Philippines. In the same breath, he would also claim to be of the upper classes. Fake it until you make it. Everybody nodded, impressed, except for me, who looked away. One girl would introduce me to her Italian boyfriend as someone from the province, not the capital, with a dismissive air as if living in the centre made her of better stock, and living far away from it made you less. She was proud to be from Parañaque, the capital of suburbia, home of the biggest subdivision in Asia. I wish I had lied too, been creative at self-reinvention in the Middle Kingdom. I would sometimes pretend I was from Jakarta until someone actually stopped to ask me about the city in detail. The opposite would happen, the more honest I was, the more it was suspected as fabrication. Or was it because I didn't see myself the way they saw me? People wanted to hear what they already believed instead of being convinced otherwise. It was too much effort.

\*

Distances began to be measured by the number of subway stops it took to get there. There was a distinct Eau de Subway scent best described as unwashed laundry mixed with metallic soot and five-spice powder. Even when blindfolded, the nose knew I was at the Xujiahui station where I lived nearby, a popular destination for gadgets and haggling. It was two stops away from work. Like everything there, the choices were dizzying, multiplied by space and numbers of floors. The abundance of choice made a problem of making a choice. What shoes would you wear if you had to choose from one hundred pairs? Shopping centres shone bright, shaped like abandoned temples or forgotten toys. A dome wedged between two buildings looked like a pronged jewel. The photos I took glowed. It was hard to see darkness in the night when artificial light was brighter than the real.

The office where I worked overlooked People Square, once teeming with Americans and its Race Club. Shanghai was an upstart compared to the rest of China but a modern one that took advantage of its growth, its colonial past spread like layers of gouache, still partly seen and experienced. The French, the Americans, the British, the Germans, each one layer after the other. They did not bleed but lay on top of colours like pages of a book. My Chinese-Spanish friend, B, who called me Hosephine, would get married in the restaurant on top of a race club with a clock tower that showed its first time in another era when Americans ruled the city. From there, you looked out at the vast spread of monuments of Shanghai: the Shanghai Museum, Grand Theatre, and the Urban Planning Exhibition Hall. The memorial we would often go to was for alcohol called Barbarossa, a Morrocan-style bar built on a lagoon in the same park where we would gather for happy-hour drinks. The minor roads from the main square reached out to where art-deco buildings designed by László Hudec from the 1920s stand as reminders of a past before a republic in 1946. The Samsung signage on top of the Nanjing shopping street became a marker for personal geographies. It was a view I would look at for almost four years. The sky was always blue from where I sat at a desk overlooking the park because one picks the stories you want to live with, don't you? In truth, there were more clogged skies and muggy air that made the throat itch. I told myself to remember the best of it and forget the rest. There were the times when shoes were spat on by strangers (the guttural sound of a clearing throat was a warning before impact) or when you were run over by bikes and motorcycles as a matter of course, or even unluckier, your bike would get stolen four times until you gave up the idea of riding altogether. The first time I had a spot of saliva dripping down my shoes, I knew I had been Shanghai-ed.

*

Visitors to the 'Hai, as some foreigners liked to call it, were taken to Nanjing Lu. These were wide avenues packed with touristy amusement and temptations: the sugar-dipped fruits, the swirling bright lights, the shops, the mini-trains, the buzz towards the stretch to the east of Nanjing Lu, towards the Bund. To find your bearings and know your place, was to look to the east. Directions in Mandarin began in the east then south onwards to the west and north or *dong, nan, xi* and *bei*. One continued to walk towards the shopping street to find the Shanghai First Food Store; there was no second food store. Here tourists went to the requisite stop for gifts to bring back home packs of candied fruit, mooncakes, vacuum-sealed duck, dried mushroom and walnuts still in their shells. Noise, chaos and abundance of food were considered good omens for a happy business. Silence was awkward, tragic and sad like sitting at a funeral. Beware the quiet dim sum place, where you can hear the echo of your voice. Down the road, you would pass by a clothing store, Clio Coddle, in neon lights, with a logo of a green crocodile with no legs. It looked familiar, like the t-shirt brand favoured by tennis players. Trademark and copyright laws were regularly flouted here as if they were mere suggestions, was anything real?

The end of Nanjing Lu was a view of the Waitan or the Bund, a row of art-deco buildings built in the jazz period of Shanghai history, one shared and shaped by outsiders. The view of the Huangpu River framed by Pudong and Waitan was a reason to catch your breath no matter what feelings you had at the moment while living there. The first image as exhilarating as the last. Something drew me to the water, however, polluted it might have been.

*

Childhood was a time of no water, although it was a happy one. There was a wayward memory of almost drowning in a pool. Up until then, I had never lived in a place with the language of rolling waves, where the river was visited and marvelled at. My memories of rivers would be connected to sites seen in China. When I would get lost and scared while travelling many years after, I would catch myself asking in Mandarin instead of English because it was the only other foreign language I knew. Angeles City was landlocked on an elevated plane built on the debris of an angry volcano that spewed ash more than five centuries ago. The nearest body of water to our house was the Abacan River, which was more of a runway of water than a river before it would be overrun by soil, drought and settlers that one forgot why it was ever called such. Evergreen fields of flatness were what I had known then, later on, it would be lahar, when I thought of home and water. Lahar was the mudflow of volcanic ash, a river that destroyed and hardened to concrete when it stood still. In Manila, water meant bay sunsets, which seemed even in childhood memories, far from the Apo St in Quezon City of my grandparents. The floods of España Boulevard were nearer. People found it strange that I could live in an archipelago and not know how to swim. They asked if I swam all day and lived in a nipa hut like the ones inside souvenir bottles labelled with the word: Philippines.

*

Crystals form in the air when water and temperatures drop before they combine with other crystals to make snow. It snowed for the first time in seventeen years in Shanghai in 2008. A surprised city looked up and saw ice dripping from the sky in flakes then pellets. The first snowfall of my life, to touch something so delicate that it would melt on my open palms like kisses. A German friend surprised at our delight would ask me, you've never seen snow? I would reply with, well, you've never been to the beach? Cars skidded on iced roads; trains stopped running. On the sidewalk, flakes turned into muddy slush. News reports advised us to be careful, to stay in and watch the snow from behind closed doors, but how could you not imagine stepping out, feeling the powdery cold. So we took photos, made snow people, lay on the ground and flapped our arms up and down to make earthbound angels. There is a photo of me holding a ball of snow shaped by gloved hands, standing beside a bike, grinning, while snow fell around me. I am underdressed for the weather with a t-shirt and a windbreaker, but it would not matter. Walking around the city, I could tell the person was from the tropics by the way they dressed for winter as if they were on an expedition to Antarctica, complete with fur-lined ear mufflers and boots. I know this because I am guilty of the same. The cold came in winds and negative numbers, crept inside living rooms with no heated floors until they gripped you even from under the covers. Survival meant staying close to heat lamps and hugging padded clothing.

*

Even when met with disbelief, I admitted to not being able to swim, which other expats would find strange because I lived on an island nation. I would learn how to swim after leaving China, long after living with the fear of drowning. I almost died as a child in a pool. Water scared me for most of my life; I tried dipping my face in a basin of water—even that was frightening. (This is a joke, but I knew someone who did. ) There was a memory of water choking me, pushing me down to make me disappear.

My uncle, an undertaker, the last blurry image as I sank and the one who would save me from drowning. In my mother's family, you knew the end was near when Uncle J began hovering silently in the background. He was called for the rites of the dead, a consultant for the best-looking coffin to please the living because the dead don't care. Gold in that patina would be flashy, he would say. Funeral paraphernalia littered my grandparent's house; a hearse was parked in the spacious garage. He bought heavy Baroque bronze and silver candelabras at auctions based on old issues of Architectural Digest. I know this because I tried to carry one out of the house. He would bury his mother, father, uncle, cousin, brother, friend, and my mother. To learn to swim then was to face the fear of drowning and the shame of being the oldest and most afraid during classes. The swimming teacher taught us to float by hitting the curling up into a ball when we jumped into the pool then lie with the water on our back as if you were opening a book. He said the water would carry us, make us buoyant, especially seawater. He spoke softly to the girl whose fear was sinking in her attempts to float. We should not be afraid to drown, he said.

\*

I would plan a trip back to China in 2013 after leaving for good in 2010. It was the year when sixteen thousand pigs clogged the Huangpu River, tainting the city's drinking water. Friends wrote back to say they were afraid of contamination. A porcine massacre. Instead of being buried, the diseased carcasses were dumped en masse by pig farmers from a border city located upstream of the Huangpu, turning the water into a bloody river, says media reports. Slimy, green swine soup. The pigs were smeared in soil, their pink flesh rotting and leaking fluids back to the river that gave them life. On and on for miles from leafy Wusong River, they floated to the Huangpu in protest of pointless deaths, their presence a reminder of rot and disease. It would not be the first time I would hear of pigs causing chaos. I once saw pigs running away in the North Luzon Expressway while driving to Manila when the truck that had carried them had turned over to its side. The driver was chasing after the pigs, frantic, taking care to lead them back to the sidewalk so they would not get hurt. Some pigs were able to bolt to freedom while others were caught again. I dreamt that night that the thousands of pigs did not die. They fled from a destiny of being made into dumplings, *hong shao rou*, and *char siu* escaping from the thousands of mouths that would gnaw at their flesh. Man versus pig, pig versus river. The river has more time than I do. I wished my mother had escaped her death and the others who died while I was away: a grandfather from a heart attack and an uncle from a speeding truck. I was not there when they passed. Here I was instead standing along the Huangpu in a dream, the river clear like a mirror reflecting the sky while watching the hundreds, then thousands of pigs swim past me in reverse. Backward they went like an unwinding clock. They stared at me with their piggy eyes, snorting a greeting, their tagged ears flopping to their faces, and their hooves thrashing in the water. If only they could, they would have walked out of the river that wanted to drown them, jumping off track from the current, and then able to walk on dry land. But they didn't kill these pigs who would escape, they swam against current, against logic, against choices made against them, trying to make it back, back upriver.

# Class Triple-A

*(noun\'klas aaa\): A term used in the counterfeit industry to grade the quality of a fake product. Class AAA means it is a good copy of the original but not a replica. These goods look like the original while being made of cheaper material.*

I called her Isla Bonita behind her back. We agreed to meet at her townhouse in the French Concession so we could go together to the shop. It would be a weekend afternoon on a scenic spring walk, taking a favourite route around the city. The Vichy government modelled the French Concession after Champs Elysees, which I thought to be hyperbole because how could a place copy another, one near me and another far, far away. But squint, and it did look like Paris from the sidewalks with its leafy London plane trees lining the road and the turn-of-century architecture before the Mandarin graffiti and faded, pokey laundry against red brick jolted the landscape.

In the city's youth, divisions by settlements followed the arriving colonials: the British, French and Americans. We would walk across these divisions to pass by the Soong mansion, home of the sisters who would marry the men to change the country, Chiang Kai Shek and Sun Yat Sen. The sisters' letters kept under glass case were penned in neat cursive script in perfect American cadence like the well-bred private school girls they were. We kept going following directions to a narrow street, up a staircase into the second floor of a dark, art-deco building. A bald man in a white shirt and pants answered Isla Bonita's knock. He let us in a brightly lit apartment of three rooms; maybe two, it made no difference because what you saw was the same. There were ceiling-to-floor shelves crammed with bags. You knew it was counterfeit because of the way they were shoved against one another like books, wasting no space between them. It was not the first time I would enter a store that dealt in real fakery, one of honest dishonesty. Copies were being sold with real ones in the open, even in subway stations, for all to see. There were places in the city where you could buy nothing real imaginatively called the fake markets. It was part of the quintessential tourist experience to be a phony goods buyer in a real city — intellectual theft in the age of mechanical reproduction. The counterfeits had permutations made of features the original inventors never even thought of — the phone with a fan, the camera with a magnifying glass. There was no hiding what they were doing, and people knew what they were buying: a prop for a life they dreamed of having where they could believe and let other people see their delusions. There were so many they displaced the real by their sheer numbers.

I was surprised she brought me here. It was beneath her. She had the trappings of the leisure class: an exceptional talent to look poreless and beautiful, a society editor-approved address, sterling overseas education, a mother who collected silver tea sets, and a father who patiently watched the stock market rise and fall as he clipped bonsai branches in their community garden club. I knew who she was because she made no effort to hide it. When we met, every syllable of her last name was enunciated, after which she paused to smile as if waiting for the letters to pop and float overhead. I thought I had gone deaf; I did hear it. I knew who she was. During my first job out of university, I worked in public relations, clipping media coverage for the boss when mileage from tony clients gained traction. She would make her famous last name known when talking to fellow Filipinos, not a habit she practised when it came to foreigners. Sartre wrote, hell was other people. You could also say hell was your countrymen because you are continually bound by their knowledge of you based from home. I knew this about her when I asked if being president of the garden club meant her father had moringa trees and coconuts in their backyard like we did. She laughed, patted my head like one would of a toy dog, and changed the subject. They also owned an island, the reason why I called her Isla Bonita. Maybe the island was self-sufficient like her, free to do as it pleased. It was her first year in China, too, working in finance. I imagined her standing on the *isla*, arms wide open, barnacles on half-sunk terrain — all this, all hers — during low tide, the shoreline memories of a succulent youth surfaced before it was reclaimed by the sea again. With her eyes closed to feel the sun on her face, I wondered, did she ever think: What did I do to deserve this life?

*

We had met at a weekend volunteering club for foreigners in Shanghai. I knew no one in the big city beyond the ones I met during Sunday mass, so I made it a point to go out and meet new people without the need to shout over club music or spend a ransom in cocktail drinks. I was an introvert hoping to be adopted by an extrovert. That weekend's event was held at a Chinese orphanage to care for kids and paint the playroom. The place looked like a kindergarten school when we were led to a room full of children. The room had white walls with vibrant blue flowers, tinted glass windows and low wooden tables and chairs. On the floor, were scattered toys and books. The smell was of dried saliva and vomit.

It was not my first time to visit an orphanage. There was wailing and the sound of continuous crying until I realized, taking a closer look, that the children were either physically disabled or mentally challenged. One boy was blind, and another was one-armed while some would not look you in the eye as they spun in place or jumped up and down. Parents abandoned the children here for being tainted copies of themselves. Otherwise, no healthy baby would be unaccounted for in China's 2008 one-child policy. Save for one. There among the little boys was a girl playing alone. She wore a pink ruffled dress, and her round cheeks were flushed from the cold. She looked like a doll you wanted to take home. There was nothing wrong with her except for being born a girl in a society that still prized boys. I was trying to feed a toddler who would not stop banging his head on the table as rice dribbled from the side of his mouth. The moderator, frustrated at the lack of progress, grabbed the spoon from me and shoved the food into his mouth without pause, forcing him to swallow or choke. The boy struggled and cried, making the other children upset until the girl also began to howl. My face crumpled while water softened the cheeks when I heard someone speak in a language I knew from the end of the room — it was Isla Bonita.

*

She began grabbing the bags on the shelf, randomly without even looking at the brand or the colour. The store had no signage from the street not because of what they sold but because what they sold was too real. It was better than Class AAA found in the fake markets. The bags had serial numbers with certificates made with a material that matched the original. They stopped being copies and became replicas; the fake supplanted the real. We were the only buyers except for a Spanish man dressed in baggy jeans and chains in serious conversation with the salesman. I remembered an article in a newspaper: counterfeit goods were used by gangs to clean dirty money. She held a yellow clutch with a crystal-studded skull:

> What do you think?
> Is it different? Sort of a memento mori?
> What is memento mori?
> Oh, that other one looks nice too!

The bags looked the same to me. Inside every new one was the same thing, space to hold your belongings. Humans wouldn't use bags if we had pouches like kangaroos. She knew the bags by heart and gave a litany: the quilted, the studded, the woven, the croc, the chained. You would not expect this from her, she of the many food allergies. No gluten, no cheese, no rice, nothing white, she said while eating four cheese pizzas. One almost killed her: After applying a facial cream costing hundreds of American dollars, her throat began to constrict. She knew it was anaphylaxis as she crawled to the bedroom to get medicine that would save her as she started swelling like fast-ripening fruit. Having heard this story, while relieved that nothing serious happened, I could not help but think of a headline since I was working as an editor for a publishing house then: Filipino Socialite Dies from Face Cream in China.

She chose more bags in the shop and asked me to make sure they were real leather. I was here not to shop with her, not really, but to help with the haggling. I said, *zhe ge bao zhende pifu?* The man laughed. I asked if the bags were of human skin. Yes, genuine leather, he said while giggling and touching his skin, as if not being able to help himself. No offense taken, accustomed as I was to being laughed at for my bumbling Mandarin. Some would make an effort to listen patiently to the tones while I spoke while others would brush it off and not bother at all or outright laugh at a foreigner sounding funny speaking their language. You must learn the art of bargaining more so when prices varied by how much money the seller can extract from you. This is a tricky dance that can get exhausting when it escalates to debate and insult when both you and the seller think you are being treated for a fool when all you want to buy is a pair of socks. Not to insist on slashed prices, and you are scolded by other people for having been conned.

Of course, there are places where you are not allowed to bargain like in the malls, theatres, or a grocery shop. One is at the Avocado Lady at Wulumuqi Lu, where attempts to get it cheaper were swatted away like flies as she recited how much less expensive it was compared to other shops selling heavily taxed goods to foreigners. Others would copy her business, also selling products specifically for *laowai*, yet no one would be like her who remembered her loyal buyers even after years when they stopped going. We called her Avocado Lady because she was the only one who sold a reliable supply of avocados, prized for Western-type dishes like breakfast food, desserts, and guacamole.

In the end, Isla Bonita bought three large cargo boxes of bags for the whole family, the entire Tatler-featured unit.

I imagined the perfumed set of the gated enclaves of Forbes and Dasmariñas sitting in their neo-colonial style church, air-kissing while on their shoulders, and manicured hands were masterpieces of Guangzhou couture. Even if they could afford it, they wanted the image without paying the price. Luxury, in the end, was manipulating perceptions. There would be no wizened European artisans leaning on a well-worn desk taking care to stitch each centimetre of vegetable tanned leather, but Chinese workers crammed, slumped low, and smoking in a factory where no sunlight came in. I was alarmed she would do this.

> Can't they tell it is fake?
> People won't ask me about it because they know I am rich. I can always say it's from my father.

True. Isla Bonita had not bought anything real since college. People would not dare question her about it for fear of sounding rude and stating the obvious. There I was part of the fooled audience. Some people preferred to be deceived and not to be told the truth. Isla Bonita was in her late 30s by then, independent and sophisticated, the type of person who would know what to say in every situation with unflappable ease. I described her that way because of who I was then: mopey, penny-pinching, blandly dressed, and still unsure about many things. Authenticity was belief. Was the other stuff in her townhouse real too? Or did I expect them to be real? The Scandinavian furniture, the oak window panels, and the signed paintings on the brick walls of the *shikumen*, a renovated lane house. Were they pretend too? Before we left, she gave me a bucket bag printed with initials, not in my name as a thank you. It was embarrassing to use as if I were afraid of being found out as an impostor, of wanting something above the pay grade, a fake. I put the bag to good use as a lunchbox where it carried my favourite thing of all: chicken adobo rice.

*

I could not look down on her copyright sins without admitting to my own. I bought fake books from men peddling a library's worth on wooden carts pushed on the street. The books ranged from bestsellers to obscure titles of war reportage. One of the things sorely missed were bookstores. Chinese ones were massive — five floors of books were not unusual — but I could not read any of them, and the heart would ache with longing, seeing pages and pages of words I could not understand. Something I would share with the neighbourhood tea shop lady who, while knowing the best concoctions for herbs and leaves, did not know how to read or write Mandarin. Buying English books from bookstores catering to foreigners meant paying ruinous prices. The transgressions didn't end there. I also bought fake DVDs from the shop at Dagu Lu after work. When celebrities back home were embroiled in a sex video scandal, the incriminating clips promptly sold on Shanghai streets. There seemed to be no censors when it came to international sex imports. Looking back now to where that shop was on the map, a little dot forgotten, I marvelled at how many steps it took and how much of it was possible in a city with sidewalks. Ask a local how far a destination was from where you were, and the answer was *hen jin*, which meant very near. The size of the country meant the concept of distance was measured and experienced in wider berths than usual. A thirty-minute stroll was considered near, and maybe when you reached the next town, only then would it be called far.

The shop sold DVDs that looked real because of the quality and breadth of selection. What did the word genuine even mean when everything was made in China? It was the maker of the world's world. The 'real thing' became harder to distinguish from what was a copy because it was both an imitation and an original being rolled out on the same production lines along with its less-exclusive kins. The store classified DVDs by actor, genre and country. They could have downloaded the whole history of cinema into that one room. You could name an obscure French movie, and amazingly it would be there as if they contained the archives of cinema itself. Did film critics hide behind their walls? It was part of a network of spaces where foreigners could gather, relieved that they had a place to hide with letters they could read, not needing to translate characters in their heads that made them feel helpless and alone. It was here that I would earn a primary education in Hong Kong mob movies.

Beijing censors banned one movie that piqued my curiosity; I didn't want to risk attention, was it worth the trouble to see? At dinners, where we talked about living in China, the night would wear on, and the topic would turn to the news of foreigners dying in the mainland for breaking laws or whispered stories on how organs were harvested from prison inmates then sold to the highest bidder. One long-time Filipino resident would make the trip to Chengdu to use his *guanxi* to try to save two Filipinos accused of stealing. He would fail. Those were the years when Filipinos were caught in Pudong Airport as drug mules, a lot of them tricked or taken advantage of, their faces and crimes splashed all over government media before they transferred to death row. No different from the treatment of Chinese caught in NAIA airport in the Philippines except those were drug syndicate members, not desperate penniless couriers, and later on, they would be jailed, released or deported not killed.

Was a banned DVD worth the aggravation? Worth risking the stare of a CCTV camera pointed at me from the ceiling? The dilemma went on in my head for weeks until, one day, I would blurt it out and ask for *Yihe Yuan* or the Summer Palace. The cashier gave a blank look as she led me to the back of the shop where they kept the Oscar-winning titles. She then proceeded to unlock a wooden box below where more boxes would be moved out until she handed the forbidden movie about a summer park in the Forbidden City. She did not even ask me why I wanted to see it. *Yihe Yuan* was about a doomed love affair that begins during the student riots of Tiananmen Square and banned for its nude scenes. Like most Chinese movies

I would watch during those years, it ended with sad longing — no one was allowed to be happy. After each trip to the shop, I would walk by a Cantonese restaurant on the street owned by the Hong Kong star, Carina Lau, who made a mint opening dance clubs in the mainland. It was not her I was interested in but the man she married in Bhutan, Wong Kar Wai muse, and actor, Tony Leung. On its wall was his signature, what if by dumb luck he was there? I imagined that if I did see him, I would cup my hands as if to whisper a secret like he did in the last scene of *In the Mood for Love*. Tony would be startled seeing a girl with lips to the glass like a janitor fish. I am a crazy fan that way.

*

The time I knew Isla was as short-lived as the autumn months. Having her in your life was like cooking risotto, you could not do anything else but watch the pot, stir the rice and ladle soup one cup at a time until the grains puffed. She was unlike other friends who behaved more like potted cactus, the friendship blooming even with little watering. She latched on like a needy child asking me to do errands for her not because she could not speak the language but because she couldn't be 'bothered to learn it'. This helplessness included even simple things like making an effort to say *Keka-kele* to ask for Coke. In the beginning, I felt sorry for her because I knew how it felt like to be new and frustrated that even meeting someone who spoke your language was a lifeline. It was like the time I met someone who had stayed in China for two decades and gave me a pitying look when he found out I had arrived that week. Why would your family let you go, he asked. Duties for her included asking for water: *Ta yao mai yiping shui.* Or talking to the *ayi* on the phone hired to clean her house: *Ni hui yun yifu ma?* To get her home in a cab: *Women yiqi da che, xian song ta zai song wo.* In a restaurant, she had me tell the waiters of her aversion to eggplants: *Ta dui qiezi guomin.* I was a gopher though, in exchange, she would be nice treating me like a younger sister you had to bribe with alcohol and food. One desperate time, I made the trek outside in zero degrees weather to her house to adjust the heater because she could not read the Chinese characters. I was glad to help someone not freeze to death. When it came down to it, I wanted to be needed and useful, an upper hand to have something that someone else wanted, in a place that would go on without me.

Shanghai was the type of place where everything and anything could happen in one night because we were foreigners looking in. She and I were bored passengers in a carriage forced to talk to each other. We knew no one else. So much of being away is living with loneliness knowing you are not home and the exhaustive effort to reconcile the language in your head with the language outside it. Geography and convenience became a basis for companionship. What was true friendship, and what was pretend? The copy and the actual? If we had met in Manila, I doubt that she would even talk to me much more invite me to dinner to meet family. She was a Class AAA friend with the lines and trappings of what looked like a friendship, felt like a friendship, but was imitation made to pass for the real deal, and maybe that was okay for the time we met, it was what was needed. And if she was one to me, perhaps I was a Class AAA friend to her too. We were interested in different things and were opposites that I was not surprised when I heard from her less and less as the months wore on as she met more new people to show her around the city. I did miss her because she was genuinely fun to be with having the unfiltered honesty of someone who already became who she was meant to be. It was flattering she turned to me to navigate the city with her, but it was a relief to no longer be the chief amateur translator for her world. I could be a foreigner in peace in mine.

*

The Mandarin word for fake is *jiade*. I learned to say this when a vendor refused to accept a *renminbi* note I offered in payment. He shook his head and pointed to it, saying it was *jiade*. Fake. Not real and unacceptable. I would keep the note as a reminder of what *jiade* meant. The paper was thinner, the indentations and watermarks fainter. Mao's face on the currency was blurry as if looking back at me behind a glass wall. I refused to be tricked again. What else was tampered with? I would see a *tai tai* wifey swathe in logos and wonder: Was what she was wearing real? An Italian sports car could be parked in front of a restaurant for a marketing blitz, yet, open the hood, and it ran on Japanese parts. In 2008, six babies died, and hundreds of thousands sickened when local milk formulas were found to have high levels of toxic melamine used in plastic and fertilizer. The milk was not milk for babies but a way to line pockets. Even years after, fear will still make parents buy imported baby milk. What did I know for sure? The grey sky was not fake; it was always grey, that I knew as I sat at my office desk overlooking People's Square watching a drowned sunset every day. A fake sky would be blue; a fake sky is only blue on television, not in real life.

People wondered if I was a *huayi* or an overseas-born Chinese because of a fair complexion and a full, round face. In the Philippines, I would never be mistaken for being a foreigner. Still, abroad, the assumption was Malaysian or Indonesian or Vietnamese or Singaporean or Chinese before they guessed that I was Filipino. I would go to mass on Sundays for the reason that I could hear Tagalog spoken around me. There, I was initially ignored, thought of as another Asian. They were surprised when I spoke Tagalog and said *ako rin* to mean me too. A taxi driver would tell me, 'You do not look like Manny Pacquiao or Gloria Arroyo'. It was the years Arroyo would visit the mainland often to court investments. They described her to me as formidable, as *hen lihai* for being a president, a petite woman with a mole. He hasn't seen enough Filipinos to know we all look different. How Chinese was I? I would answer that I was Filipino with no Chinese blood.

One of my great, great, great, great, great, great, great, great ancestors was Chinese in the 18th century, did that count? I would say as a joke to new friends who would not even smile to be polite.

It puzzled me that being Chinese came in percentages measured in blood, not by choices. Did they go to a temple? What did they eat? Did they have an altar for their elders? It was the choices you made every day. One friend liked to say that he was the real Chinese Filipino being exactly 50 per cent Filipino and 50 per cent Chinese. Another would say that he estimates he is 30 per cent Chinese because his half-Filipino father married a Filipina. One acquaintance, who was mistaken for not being Chinese enough because of her round eyes and light hair, would defend herself, saying she was 100 per cent pure Chinese. We go to the temple, she would reason. I would never understand how it feels like to choose between two cultures because I am not an immigrant. The people I had met then were either second- or third-generation ethnic Chinese who grew up with strong ties to the Philippines while also keeping contact with relatives in the mainland. They considered themselves to be both; it was possible to choose an 'and' and not be punished for the tyranny of one.

Looks can also be faked. I began to notice eye folds and wondered how I would look like if my eyelids had no folds or what they called a *ting sun*. They put thin transparent stickers on their lids to create folds through careful placement and patience. Huge, Western-shaped eyes were judged more beautiful, and lighter skin shades were preferred. It sounded like a lot of effort to someone like me who forgets to brush her hair. Word got around if you had your eyelids sliced. One pointed out a girl across us who had her eyes done. She had agreed to a *ting sun* for life for a measly sum charged by a medical student in Shenzhen. To do it, she lied to her whole family. By the time they had found out it was already done, her eyes bandaged, and she lay waiting for a week in bed praying for perfect eyelids. The operation made her eyes bigger, fuller, more curious. Asian, but not Chinese. I wished she did not think of me as rude for staring at them while wondering if she liked herself more. Did she look a stranger even among her family? Was it her unconscious way of rebelling against what she was born with?

*

The last time I would hear from Island Girl again was when she left the city for good. We stopped meeting. I would catch glimpses of her in the peripheries of social life: at parties or across a restaurant or a bar. We would wave a shy hello or I called out her name over the din. One time, it was a greeting over a moving subway door. In between, there was talk of coffee that never happened. Word spread how her years in the mainland amounted to boxes and boxes of objects that she could not bring herself to get rid of, which included, among the other random things one accumulates in China, a bamboo bike and a robot panda. It was through this network and a common friend, she sent me a package: a rolled-up oil painting.

I knew the work at once, having seen it hung on the bathroom vanity of her home. It was a pastel-hued painting of a bucolic field done in an expressive, impressionist style. A backlit, sunlit glow diffused the farming landscape with colours in sincere homage to painter Fernando Amorsolo's chiaroscuro technique yet missing the mark. In the middle of the canvas was a couple standing beside each other smiling while in a tight embrace. Unsigned. I doubted it was valuable but guessed that it was not a cheap copy. Maybe it was something she liked on her own without considering the opinion of others or how it would reflect on her status. She had the habit of displaying the signed ones in the living room where the names could be gawked at by visitors. The painting was both a copy and an original piece of work like the Class AAA bags she bought all those years ago. It was a league of its own, a sweet parting gift knowing I would like it. She did remember me even after all these years. Those weeks of buying bottled water and memorizing the words for cleaning her townhouse were not unnoticed. I thought, Island Girl stared at this while sitting on the toilet, a vulnerable moment, unguarded and not set out to impress. The thought made me smile. At last! Something real.

# Dispatches From a Past Life

## #1 Metro stop pause

The goal was to blend in by not calling attention to yourself. That is to breeze through, with your head pointed straight ahead, not allowing chance curiosities to catch you off guard like a bouquet of glitter or the long line for milk tea. Committing metro stop entry and exit points to memory were habits that made you feel like a local. Don't gape at signs, scratch your head, or raise your voice when asking strangers for directions. In the beginning, it was frustrating to play charades for basic needs like shampoo, not lotion, chicken breast, not rabbit. But soon, those sounds turned to meaning when characters began to count for something. As a commuter, it meant knowing that to enter was said as *jin ru* with the logograms looking like a pound sign on a slide beside another with two stick legs striding. Exit was *chu kou* which looked like an upturned spider scrambling beside a square, which meant a mouth.

From People's Square to Caoxi Lu station, it was up
the stairs leading to Exit #4. I was glancing up at the same
upturned spider on the sign at the Caoxi metro stop where
I got off to go to the IKEA store, far from downtown.
I was there to accompany Pikachu to help furnish a new
flat along with a group of friends who helped her haul off
things in a rented van. She disliked waste and always saw
gold in found objects which was not far from her profession
in finance and squeezing values from gross figures, inflated
values and depressed assets. I wondered why we got along
when on paper we shouldn't have; then I remembered it was
her who pointed me to the direction of which museums to
visit. I began to double-step while in a hurry, mind filled
with the worries of the day. IKEA would be a quick walk
from the station. Under the fading afternoon light, I saw
him. There was a Uighur man ahead of me with a little
square cap, a *doppa*. I knew he was Uighur because of his
features, the tall patrician nose, dark eyes and the ethnic
clothing. He was smoking a cigarette with his sleeves rolled,
seemingly relaxed as if on a lazy stroll. I walked behind him
and thought Pikachu should be there by now. The man
then stretched his arm to reach out to the woman in front
of him, a short blond girl who looked like a tourist because
of what she was wearing, to pull down the main zipper of
her backpack. He was a pickpocket! Shanghainese talked
about petty crime committed by Uighurs like they were a
nuisance, flies buzzing around with no mention or context
of the 're-education' camps where they were tortured or the
systematic oppression they endured as a minority. Why did

they have to leave and go here in the first place, so far away from home. This was also years before the government would intensify efforts to erase their culture in a series of programmes that flouted human rights. I would know about these details after leaving from a friend who was advised that the best way to help the Uighurs was to do it from outside China. I was not alone walking behind him and there were others who were walking past. Couldn't they see it? I could not decide whether to call for help, make noise or do both. What about the unsuspecting girl? The Uighur man? What would police do to him? Or do I let it go because I am a foreigner in a Communist country? I knew of Uighurs because they sold cheap delicious food: hand-pulled noodle dishes, grilled lamb kebabs on the sidewalk, *yang rou chuan*, sprinkled with cumin and spices. I would watch as I sat on a rickety wooden chair and folded my arms on plastic-covered tables as they would stretch, stretch, stretch noodles puffed with flour until they were folded into a bowl with sauce and vegetables. The Uighurs were Muslim, a persecuted minority from Xinjiang, to the westernmost part of China under Communist rule since 1949. They were closer in culture to the Stans than they were to the Chinese. I have never seen a Uighur be anything else but a food vendor or a restaurant owner. It seems these are the only roles they are allowed to play. There was a moment's pause between when I saw him smoke and with two fingers open a bag zipper as if he were sketching a half-moon. I kept walking and before I could react, it was the girl who was being pickpocketed who made the decision for me. She felt movement behind and shifted her head to scream before her wallet was fished out like the catch of the day. Instead of panicking, the man looked at her shocked face, arms in a defensive stance and simply walked past as a trail of smoke lingered over his head.

## #2 Balikbayan boxes

They called it repatriation boxes with sizes depending on how much you wanted to send back home. Space never seemed enough. The boxes could go home when the sender could not. It was love sent from a distance. So it was a box meant to represent the presence of a loved one and to distract from the longing with the promise of better things. It was my first time to assemble one, having been at the receiving end of those boxes for many years. Phone calls would be made asking if it had arrived. To gather around a box as its top was ripped had become a ritual. Family anticipated its opening with a mix of curiosity, anticipation and self-interest by making sure they were not left out. I began to appreciate the effort it took to carefully fill stuff into the corrugated cardboard box to be sent through a Filipino I met at church. There were new rubber shoes for a sibling, teas, curtains for the house, small tokens for an extended family tree and an assortment of things that could be found in the factory of the world, all carefully locked in place inside like playing the video game Tetris. I was not confident enough with my Mandarin to look for a shipper myself. The shipper was a Filipino we referred to as the Unofficial Mayor of Shanghai because he seemed to be everywhere: in church and bars, hosting parties, grinning at the corner of press photos at big-ticket events in a black suit trying hard not to be noticed. After Sunday mass, he could be seen at the centre of a crowd laughing because he made sure to know the new arrivals to the city because of the shipping package business that he ran on top of being a manager at a catering company. He was one of the few people I knew who could scold and curse his whole staff in Mandarin. No one could be sure if he were Asian or not, his features were European even Arabic. It was only confirmed when you heard him speak. Those were the years when we were younger and horrible things did not happen or not yet. Accidents were for people you read in newspapers or online not for your reality though to work abroad was to allow another type of box that used the word, repatriation, to apply. The box used to return the remains of the dead, of a body hit by a car, a body abused or beaten up or if not a box, a person invalidated by illness now facing repatriation.

## #3 The Lai Lai Club

There are places in the city I've never been to and could not go to but would see through the eyes of others. One of those people was Kenji, a Japanese journalist I met for the first time during a hotpot dinner on a winter night. I presumed he was with his boyfriend then, by the way they wore the same clothes as if mirroring one another, each the half of a coupled whole. Kenji wrote for a business magazine and in his spare time wrote stories about Shanghai's aging

population. He would talk to dozens of seniors fending for
themselves, some forgotten by their one child love. For
Kenji, maybe talking to them reminded him of the parents
he left behind in Japan. We were alike in that way — both
children worried about their parents. It was because of these
stories that he would tell me about the Lai Lai Dance Club
in far-off Hongkou, near the Hongqiao airport. Two days
a week on Friday and Saturday, Lai Lai was frequented by
married middle-aged men who were allowed to show they
liked other men only on those days. Homosexuality is still
considered a mental illness in China for an older generation
that did not grow up with the internet. At the Lai Lai,
they go dancing cheek to cheek, hand holding hand, on a
spot of real estate they can dare to be. They begin facing
each other, hands stretched to the side and feet shuffling to
the left and right before they are palm to palm with arms
overhead while teeny, high-pitch Chinese songs played
on strings about failed love. Kenji told me this while on
the weekend at a mountain retreat amid a bamboo forest.
I imagined them dancing like the retired couples in the park
during the mornings, with some women swaying alone, not
caring whether they had a partner or not. These solo women
began dancing, moving in circles in time with the couples
around her. Some practised calligraphy with a cup of water,
tracing characters on black floor tiles while children looked
on. It would have been awkward for me to accompany him
there though when he began to tell his stories, in my head
I was with Kenji, climbing up the yellow-stained stairs to
the Lai Lai that night, my hand on the wooden railing and

jazz music drifting slow and long. I would scowl when I glance to see his tape recorder with him, held in his left fist. How could they talk to you if you have a recorder pointed to their faces? And a foreigner at that. A man had asked to dance with him in the middle of the ballroom surrounded by tables and couches. Kenji would nod in reply and leave behind a beer bottle. They danced in the Lai Lai for two songs before other men began giving them jealous looks. Kenji is not in Shanghai now; he left after a few years and was now studying indigenous people for grad school. I am glad to have met him and known all these stories other than my own.

## #4 Happy birthday

The first birthday in a new country is always memorable because you are not home. The weather was getting colder, much colder than we expected for winter. I spent the day in Shanghai, having dinner with friends followed by coffee. They pooled money to give me a hoodie shirt and a bag, these people I've known for a few months though the weeks felt like years. We spent time together regularly because of days unencumbered by obligations. The slate was wiped clean because there was no one else to know. The hours needed to be considered friends filled easily to the brim overflowing. Several people called on the phone from home to greet me. I was still remembered and missed by friends and family. Milk Tea smiled as she overheard me talk, and after would say how people will remember you during the first year of being away and by the next, will move on without you. This wisdom was based on her experience working in a factory in Taiwan for many years. The space in their lives I had left behind will soon be replaced by others as I replaced them with the new people I met, like water seeking its own level. When you are the one living away, it is easy to pretend those left behind will stay the same as if time back home stood frozen, and you only had to re-enter the film before it went back to running the same reel. It was okay for the exile to change yet it was harder to accept that those left behind changed too. The night ended with me taking the cab home alone, convincing myself that homesickness would pass. Some of the indelible conversations I've had were with cab drivers bored of routine, had nowhere else to go but drive, and found the novelty of speaking to a foreigner who spoke Mandarin too amusing to resist. They told me about their lives, what they thought of the city, even one time complaining why Shanghainese women refused to marry his son. The reason was lack of money. Love was not even mentioned. For this cab driver, I told him the truth: I was alone in China and it was my birthday. I am sad, I said in Mandarin knowing the simple statement would be heard. He nodded but began to smile, glancing my way to see if I was teary at the back seat. His smile had some teeth missing while the rest was stained tea-brown. He cleared his throat and began singing the words to a song. I understood! He was singing happy birthday to you, to me: *Ni de shengri kuai le, ni de shengri kuaaaaai leeee, ni de shengri kuai le.*

# #5 The Little Mermaid

For her, again I would line up for hours as if in a pilgrimage. As a child I begged my parents for money to buy the soundtrack when the Disney version of the Hans Christian Andersen classic was made into a cartoon movie with talking creatures and collections under the sea. I would know the lyrics to those songs and filled colouring books of Ariel, hair red and long with seashell bra and friends playing under a vast sea. It was a memory wrapped in the soft nostalgia of childhood, though I would wonder in my heart of hearts why Ariel gambled family, voice, home for a man she barely knew. During the World Expo 2010, she would be the main attraction at the Danish Pavilion where lines snaked and snaked until they could no longer coil. This was a first trip overseas, the first time after decades, where she would be removed from a promenade perch in Copenhagen. Hans Christian Andersen fairy tales are widely read in China since the 1930s with each translation changed depending on the times. When in a bookstore, I would flip through the pages of famous childrens' books read in English, now lost to me because it was written in Mandarin Chinese. I wondered how closely they followed the original text in the act of translation when removed from their contexts where more freedoms were enjoyed. The Little Mermaid fairy tale endured as one of the most popular. It was the reason why Chinese tourists flocked to visit the Andersen museum. The pavilion was white with circular ramps that showcased Danish products like beer and Lego as you walked deeper and deeper as if inside a shell.

Finally after standing and waiting, there she was made of bronze sitting on a boulder, naked with half-formed legs attached to a tail fin looking at a light blue pool underneath inside a walled world invaded by strangers. The Lonely Little Mermaid in China. After much anticipation, it was no surprise she fell from the high pedestal toppling down and rolling over. I thought I knew what she would look like but didn't. There was an expectation the statue would be bigger, the sight of it magical like the idea of a fairy tale and remembered childhood anticipation though in reality, it was accurately named Little Mermaid. Expectations disappointed me, not the actual. These were the years before social media would inundate one's perception of sightseeing with repeated, recreated images of embodied beliefs on what something should look like. I heard of people deciding where to go next on the map based on what kind of photo the place could give them and not by reason of making a journey or experiencing something new. The boxed view of social media was used to display the same dizzying cliff, another pearlescent sunset.

She was not Disney Ariel, no. In China, she arrived displaced, moved from the time, place and culture which made her, on that harbour in Copenhagen where she was once stolen, many times vandalized, mutilated, beheaded to being supplanted here to a white space, flown in on a business trip to represent a country; a woman working away from homeland just like me.

## #6 The 20 renminbi view

You could buy a lot with 20 *renminbi* back then: two bowls of peanut noodles on the street, notebooks at a subway stationery shop, socks, hankies. You got the picture. The 20 *renminbi* note had the face of Mao Zedong on one side and a view of the River Li on the other with the grand karst mountain landscape like humpback whales against a brown sky. Two people, one sitting down and the other standing, are on what looks like a straight line but is a raft navigating the expanse of jade water. If you held up the note to the exact point of the river where the copy on the money was made, it would be an uncanny rendered reproduction of the famous scene painted countless times in brush and ink by artists and written about by poets. Cheese planned the Yangshuo itinerary with boundless optimism for time and the energy of the Road Runner. This meant we stayed for some stops for a day or a few hours before we were whisked away to the next destination. We did not complain because we would be able to see more of Yangshuo, a town morphed into a backpacking place catered to foreign tourists travelling around China. What did I see? My letters about it recalled more. I wrote to friends where we went and sent photos of myself posing with other people in views I could not recall, but there it was, there was a photo of myself smiling and happy for the camera not knowing, years later, I would write about this trip for another person, alone, typing away towards a deadline. There is a memory of staying in a white room after 24 hours in the city to leave again early the next morning before dawn. Another is waking up from a pinewood-lined one to climb a mountain during sunrise for a friend's birthday. *Silangan* in Tagalog, to the east. It was as lovely as a golden South Sea pearl as all sunrises could be when the light is so, though this one was marred by two people in the group bickering about breakfast. They were ex-lovers who tried to be cordial. Sunrise not included. As it was with plans made with friends, some were more involved than the others. Half the group made the arrangements while the other half tagged along proudly calling themselves Team Useless for having no contribution to the trip whatsoever. In those days, even with the internet, it was a struggle to travel around China without speaking Mandarin. By the time we had arrived to see the Li River in Guilin, a bus ride away, we were silent from exhaustion and lack of sleep yet could not let the day go like a kid tugging kite strings to steer it away from pole lines. Make full use of the journey; no day must be left idle and unturned. There was an attempt to recreate the scene on the *renminbi* note. One of us took it out from his pocket to compare, holding the currency against the actual, quintessential Chinese landscape view. Why did we travel to repeat images we already saw somewhere else? Looking around, there it was, the bamboo raft similar to the one pictured as if stepping into a staged set. Even with other tourists around us, the scene made you stop on your heels. Prices were haggled and agreed on. A friend and I sat on a raft while a boatman would steer us to the length of the river. I was ready with my camera, ready to take in the view that we had travelled so far to see. Sitting on bamboo chairs, the river was still, the weather cool and the undulating mountains looked like the spine of a rare medieval animal. Despite teeming with tourists, the boatman guided us in silence that would shush me to sleep and let the camera loosen from my grip and fall on the lap. The friend beside me stopped talking to admire the view. Two hours passed. We woke up by the shoreline, the boatman still standing waiting for his tip and other friends already there. Writing it down here now to recall the blunder, I don't feel bad about it because remembering what I had missed was a chance to do it all over again.

## #7 Tragedies far from home

The worse thing about living away from family is not being there when someone you love dies. There was an escalating feeling of dread when the phone blinks and it is a number from home. It was a long-distance call, more expensive and urgent, taken in the hallway. I did not care who heard me or that the voices rose and croaked. The earliest way out of Shanghai was the next day, a three-and-a-half-hour flight. My grandfather had died the past hour, dropped dead of a heart attack at the hospital while an aunt looked and wailed. It was a quick death, as he wished. He was a doctor who kept a long list of people he loved and their death anniversaries on his work desk at home. Now, his name would be included in that list. He wanted to avoid a death that included being bedridden or immobile. In the same hour, I would get an email about being offered a job. There was elation and grief. I didn't know what to make of it: to be sad and happy at the same time. Lolo was in his '90s when he passed away, still strong, yet he must have already felt something but didn't tell us. I took the stairs in panic wanting to feel my legs move. The building supervisor asked me in Mandarin what the matter was, trying his best to comfort a crying woman. The assumption was I would be there when he passed away as I'd always been for loved ones, but the memories for that didn't exist. I had to borrow other people's version of events, of an aunt who watched him drop on the floor as he clutched his chest. There were gaps in memory filled with negative space of the months and years I lived outside the country far away from family and friends. I came back to an archive of home with files missing.

## #8 Language X-change

They called it language exchange because the premise was to swap knowledge of your native language. Lessons were expensive and this was a cheaper way to do it while meeting new people in the spirit of friendship and culture. The language exchange partner was foisted on me, literally. I had arrived early in the dorms realizing with mounting dread and anxiety, I was one of the few foreigners and an Asian one at that to speak English. There was a woman at the office who chatted with me then promptly made calls. Would I like a language exchange partner? she asked.

This was a term I heard for the first time, a day over since my arrival at university grounds. I hadn't even met the roommate, yet I was looking at the mailboxes by the lobby because I expected to receive and send letters, something people found me strange for wanting. She explained that I would learn the language faster that way. I agreed. She made more phone calls and told me to wait. It did not take a long time before I was whisked inside a car, though in hindsight, I shouldn't have gone with someone I didn't know. I was nervous where they would drive me to which was, to my relief, a newish but empty foreign hotel inside campus. Foreign. They labelled things as foreign and left the opposite of foreign, unnamed. These distinctions made itself evident early on during my stay, something with the label foreign meant it was nicer, newer, cleaner — *xifang de* — while local was dirty, noisy and cheaper. When asked to compare or make an opinion about something, the words foreign and Western were qualifiers to gauge if you had to brace yourself for a measure of hardship. Squat toilets where local, seat toilets considered to be Western and convenient. Hard-as-rock mattresses were considered local and softer beds to be Western. If you got sick, you would only be accepted at the hospital for foreigners and not a local one because of language but also facilities. Western things were being copied and shaped in their likeness but there was still a resistance to it that made it more interesting during translation because of the differences in culture and context. These distinctions would soon blur later on as the country became richer and there would be less of the contrasts present in big cities. Neighbourhood eateries were torn down and remade into approximations of a Western concept fast-food joint. It was here in the university's hotel for foreigners that we ordered a drink or rather the language exchange partner did. He was in high school, chubby in his tight shirt and NBA cap, something that he loved, basketball. I knew why they picked me. It was because I looked harmless, this Asian girl who could speak English. He ordered orange juice for both of us that he would pay for later on. It was less of a language exchange but more like a language listening. They called it language exchanges where one teaches another each other's language through casual chatting and meeting new people. Sometimes if not done well, these language exchanges became boring. I made the mistake of asking him about his family life, did he have siblings? He looked surprised, I asked, his eyes growing larger when he tried to answer the question in English saying that, no, he had no sibling. Idiot me to forget China's one-child policy! It was a question asked for people you did not know well. Their one-child wonders who were the centre of their world, which explained the determination to give him a chance to learn English. He learned more English from me than I learned Mandarin from him. He would introduce me to his parents; his mother gave me touristy trinkets like framed, embroidered renditions of the same landscape I would see repeated in trips when travelling alone or with friends.

Another language partner was C, a Hunanese who lived in Singapore for ten years and worked for an airline company.

I answered her ad for a language partner online because she wanted to meet at a place nearby where I lived. I still hadn't given up on improving my Mandarin because of the expectations and humiliation of not knowing it fluently. Her English was alright; I did not understand why she still wanted to study. I suspected it had something to do with wanting to feel less lonely in a new city. She was not from Shanghai and did not know anyone. I asked her why not make friends with Shanghainese then? But they spoke in Shanghainese language and would not want to talk in Mandarin or Hunanese with her, she said. You could not escape language even if you were Chinese. I'd hear about this before, how Chinese students living abroad would rather speak in English than Mandarin because their mother language was not the same as the national one. English made the world an articulate place for me too because I wrote and read in the language yet sadly a less varied one.

From the beginning, C was in a melancholy mood with personal troubles and regrets about living in Singapore, where she was maltreated and called a whore while walking down the street. A whore? I asked, noting how the word was pronounced in Mandarin. Her new boyfriend would break up with her soon after because of parental disapproval. His father objected to her unstable income as a freelance teacher that she would be a burden to the family by not having a regular salary. I was surprised by this lack of romance and love in potential partners but realized later on that maybe that meant more freedom and less illusions.

Don't we choose partners who are similar to ourselves economically and mentally anyway? We don't talk about it openly because it is considered taboo, and you will be judged as materialistic and crass. Love is the supposed basis of relationships when it is constant negotiation that makes it last. I would never see her again after a few meetings. She said she was sad about the broken engagement.

My next language exchange partner would be Mik, a new graduate from a local university who spent hours in their yard learning English, wondering if she would ever see the world outside China. She asked me how I knew how to speak the language, did I live in England or America? Did you have a foreign teacher in school? It's an advantage often taken for granted and something I never questioned before. She also told me something I didn't know, if I heard correctly, that she grew marijuana in her backyard. One bush, she said, was legal.

## #9 The Mao of Mao

The Mao statue stands on top of a short shelf of books, dusty from neglect. It is a small, kitschy Mao Zedong in a green-suited coat with one hand upright waving goodbye while another is clutching a hat. It was the same hat an uncle had given me one time during his first trip to China in the 1980s. The Mao statue was bought at the antique market where nothing was a relic but had the patina of age without the years for it. I purchased the statue along with a fake Shanghai watch. I knew it was fake because of its price, and it would stop working after a few months. The Mao statue I bought because it was touristy and it was a fixture in the landscape though even back then it was being threatened as new buildings and infrastructure seemed to spring up every day. Sometimes the Mao statue was standing with both hands clipped behind its back and overlooking a campus field of green or a criss-cross of roads. Or he is sitting down. Or he is waving again, but there is no hand or hat this time. Part of his coat is flipped open as if from an imaginary wind. The statue was usually found in universities if not on tourist souvenirs, that it was easy to forget the fact that Mao had once been blindly worshipped as a god. This omission was made ubiquitous when his face was on cheap shirts, bags, pens, keychains, or anything that could be made fast and chucked inside a suitcase by tourists. Whenever international students visited the university campus, they made a stop in front of the statue to have their photo taken with the gigantic version of Mao Zedong. The Mao statue itself could charge for every picture taken with him, and he would be a rich man. The first time I heard Mao Zedong in Mandarin, I had misheard the tone and thought the speaker meant 'cat' because that was also a *mao*. So what I heard in my mind was Cat Zedong.

## #10 Typhoon Ketsana

Vitriol came by email. China couldn't block emails like social media so it was through a long string of upset, angry messages forwarded from one contact to another that news about a Filipina working in the Middle-East reached me on the days after Typhoon Ketsana also called Ondoy hit. I clicked open the message. She said those who perished during the flood deserved to die because they were sinners. I read the responses and paused. Grief for the disaster turned into rage against a gloating, thoughtless woman. Why not send the fundraising letter instead? When Ketsana made landfall in the Philippines on 26 September 2009, I was going through the checklist of apartment expenses. More bills, I thought, maybe it was time to stay at home this weekend. The proxy server was down. News of a typhoon heading the country was not unusual.

I tried calling family to make sure they were out of harm's way, no one was answering. My brother then did not go home and stayed with a friend because of the news. The typhoon dumped almost 14 inches of rain in six hours in a clogged, band-aid capital held together by uneven means. No container could hold that much rain. Manila became a water world where houses drowned with only the tips of their hats peeking. A friend would post hourly photos of cars engulfed by murky water, bit by bit, in slow horror while his family watched stranded on the second floor. The water lines would stay in some houses as if they were growth rings on a tree marking where life happened before and after Ondoy. Buildings toppled. More than seven hundred people died. Handmade rafts became totems for survival and resignation to ferry one family to another, composed of cobbled together pipes bound by rope and sheer hope as glue to thin plastic sheets and coloured basins. A biscuit tin became the captain's seat. An estimated twenty typhoons visit the Philippines in a year and the names roll out the tongue marked by remembrance depending which one came closest to kill you: people in Bulacan remember Typhoon Pedring the most, Leyte for Haiyan, and Typhoon Bopha for those living in Mindanao.

Fundraisers were held to help those whose lives were affected but it still did not feel enough because you were not there. We felt empowered gathering at the Filipino restaurant, Luneta, to talk about it and worry over sizzling sisig and garlic rice thinking perhaps eating the food from home would make us feel the distance less. It would be after going back that I would be able to fill in the blanks of unbelievable images while away. A stranger would tell me how, in less than thirty minutes, in the middle of the night, they decided to leave their house with nothing but the clothes on their backs as the water continued to rise until their present life disappeared and the future was an uphill climb to safety.

# Cowboy Nights at Zapata's

A Filipino couple introduced him while I stood by the doorway as people spilled out of morning mass. Johnson knew the Philippines with the affinity of a long-lost relative arriving at a family reunion, having lived in Quezon City to study at a Jesuit university as a seminarian. A Beijinger in Shanghai for training, he had the symmetrical good looks of a movie star in a *wushu* flick or Cantonese romantic comedy. Pikachu and I were on our first year living in the city 'upon-the-sea' still not used to its stifling outdoors in the summer and icy rooms with inadequate heating in winter. It was 2008. She worked as a banker while I did editorial work for a publishing firm helping foreigners invest in China. We were, what was called, a half-pat or a half-expat, those hired directly while in the mainland and not flown in on cushy company plans. There were a lot like us. The United States financial crisis was a full-blown meltdown, depressing industries, shutting down systems. There was an influx of foreigners flying in from Europe and the United States to find jobs in China to wait it out as if taking refuge in a bomb shelter while the economies of their home countries recovered.

Johnson said more, but it was barely audible to me as the vision of him moved as if in slow camera capture. We extended our hands with blushing cheeks and toothy grins at the same time, cooing how his English was so good. Never mind that he spoke Mandarin with a heavy Beijing accent with the garrulous rrrr's mixed in that for a moment, it felt like watching a silent film and reading lips. He asked something about finding Filipino food in the mainland; I nodded, also noticing he dressed well as a boy-next-door-gee-whiz cutie. He said he would be at the church Bible study group, so we readily agreed to join as well. Our loyal attendance was because of homesickness, a place to belong for those new to the city. For those times at the end of a long week when, on top of everything else, you remained misunderstood because you could not speak the language well enough.

One learned to accept the frustration of not being able to express the full range of who you were, to be satisfied with incomplete answers to questions when if asked in another language, you would say more. You learned to bite your tongue when it came to arguments you could not win because you forgot the Mandarin terms for scam or unfair. The language beat you to a pulp even before you opened your mouth. Even then, it was always a question of how long have you lived here when they did hear you speak. How long does it take to belong to a place? One year, two years, two decades? To be called fluent was to hit the right tones, to be understood. I met an American in the subway who lived in China since the 1970s. She was still treated like a stranger because she did not look Asian. I stopped to consider how much it was even harder for her then. The church was a way to cope in another culture where you are treated as a visitor. It was here we built a small kingdom of home inside the Middle Kingdom.

Filipinos working as house staff for expatriates or managers at hotels and restaurants attended the Bible study group. They lived well with good pay and days for rest. I thought of myself able to get along with anyone, yet the reality was less than ideal. I kept quiet when they told their jokes, which sounded like dog whistles to me. I did not know how it felt like to take care of kids, not your own, or to eat strange food in a house where you were employed. They spoke in excited tones in languages I barely understood. Despite this, I felt at ease with them, welcomed. We had our universal love for food, shared tips on how to send gift boxes, and money back home. They talked about where to buy ingredients for Filipino cooking. I asked them for recipes for beef kaldereta or how to make pork sisig. More than the pleasure of staring at Johnson — googly eyed — each afternoon came with a snack of stir-fried noodles and steamed rice cakes. Some days it would be colourful desserts like *sapin-sapin* with grilled pork skewers. These were flavours taken for granted back home now relished because chicken adobo never tastes as good as when you are in a country that does not cook it.

By then, Pikachu and I were smitten by the hunky man of God in a friendly competition to vie for his attention by elbowing each other on who would say the most insightful thing to impress him. I stopped wearing eyeglasses and began to wear contacts to avoid looking nerdy, and Pikachu started to put on makeup even though she did not like the feel of it on her face.

Unlike our motivations, it was music that brought Johnson to church. The sweet fading notes of choir songs made him look for its source. He began to attend mass every day after work. Same time, the same pew was facing the same robed priest in repeated gestures timed in beat with the words of the mass. Stand up, sit down, raise your hands to the ceiling, and nod to each other as hello. The strange rituals he looked forward to as days went on gave comfort and soothed him as he cycled among the din of Beijing's narrow alleyways, not knowing what the words meant. He continued to show up. Months after, someone would ask him to join the seminary, and he would say yes.

*

A priest in the family was a ticket to heaven, so my grandmother liked to believe. Seven sons sent to the seminary in the hopes that at least one would become a priest. She went to mass each day. If my father had believed the same, I would never have been born. My father would attend for a few years and never return after a summer spent watching shows on their new colour television.

There were no television sets in the seminary. During the Martial Law years, one son would become a priest and later on renounce it to become a journalist, narrowly escaping police capture. Another would become a monk and help people hide during the People Power Revolution to join the angry crowd that would storm Malacañang Palace and find it empty of the family who once ruled it. The dictator and kleptocrat Ferdinand Marcos and his family along with Fabian Ver and Eduardo Cojuangco escaped on a helicopter to Clark Air Base before making the sunset journey to Hawaii. A good or bad thing depending on which side you were on. Good things happen to bad people, and bad things happen to good people. Where was justice in all this, in God's country? Nowhere. The helicopter did not leak, malfunction, or explode. No knife-wielding person attacked them in broad daylight, nor were they shot by a long-range bullet. Their bodies were not hung in a public square like Mussolini to be insulted and pelted by rocks and hammers. Not one of them stumbled on a sharp object to have their head accidentally impaled. They did not catch a deadly virus with no known cure. Instead, people would forget and vote for them again decades after.

As for my father, he kept in touch with boyhood friends from that time in his life and talked shop about former classmates who have gone ahead to be priests. They would gossip, forgetting someone was listening in, about a classmate who bought a sports car or rumoured to have a mistress. He would stop going to mass himself, only sometimes under duress.

My grandmother believed in miracles because she would see one in her lifetime. A dying infant son recovered overnight after doctors gave up on him, and she left him at the foot of Mama Mary's statue. It could have been that my uncle, then only several days old, was not ready to die. She would subscribe to a lifelong devotion to daily mass. The same miracle, alas, would not happen for my grandfather and, later on, mother. It was because of my mother that we attended hours-long healing masses every week. No miracle would happen. Was it because she was a bad person? I don't know. How did others survive while some did not? The nun I asked would not know either. I had seen the x-rays, the obtrusive tests. Doctors used special terms to detach themselves from a terminal case. Medical students filed into her room where they would read a record sheet, and a doctor would talk in terms we could not understand. On the forms were the words metastasized, and Stage 4 scribbled in doctorly script.

All the eggs in the world offered for granting prayers could drown Sta Clara Monastery in soufflés as tall as hills, yet during sleepless nights I knew the inevitable would come. The house was littered with religious tchotchkes from blessed handkerchiefs, medallions to salt, and even photos meant by the giver to make you feel better when it made you feel worse. It meant your case was past science's reach, and now was the time to ask for divine intervention. As I lifted my arms when the priest asked for healing, I knew faith, whatever was left of it, would not be enough to heal anyone, much more my mother. I felt guilty, what if she could tell? It didn't matter. Eyes closed in prayer, she believed, and each time it gave her respite from suffering. As I wheeled her around the chapel, I worried how she was disappearing before my eyes, as each month passed her cheeks sunk lower. The complexion became ashen as the scale dropped more and more to the left. She was told the slender frame suited her. With a chuckle, she would say in exchange for losing weight; I got death.

*

St. Ignatius Cathedral was a gothic-style red-brick church beside a subway stop. Built by the Jesuits in 1906, it was the base for the Roman Catholic Diocese of Shanghai until the 1950s. When seen from overhead, the church formed a cross with two spires at its feet, as if sending a sign. It was here Never Mary, church police reigned. A wrinkled woman bent with age yet sprightly in step she met you at the door, walked up and down the pews, and kept you in her line of vision. I see you; she seemed to say. This was the church above ground; the state registered one. There was talk of a larger underground church holding masses in secret by clergy appointed by the Vatican and not the state. Those found to swear loyalty to Rome were persecuted and imprisoned or would disappear like the early Christians. I would not try looking for the secret church held in homes though I would wonder about the split worlds cleaved in the middle beginning the Cultural Revolution on matters of faith and loyalty. The state priest — registered, numbered, accounted for — would face us every Sunday resplendent in official garb as windows streamed light, filtered in stained glass iconography. Then would the same ritual happen somewhere else in the city, another priest facing another pious crowd, their faces recognizable by electric light in a small room despite the darkness of an existence held in secret. Could Never Mary be a spy for the party? To whom did Johnson promise loyalty? I imagined he offered prayers and forgiveness to both God and the government. To one, he promised loyalty, and to the other, he asked for permission. There were rumours that CCTV cameras watched our every move, but I never looked close enough to confirm, wanting to pretend that I did not hear what I heard. I kept my head low. In the country I came from, to be Catholic was to be born into a colonial inheritance and follow the majority. In China, to be Catholic was to resist, to risk remaining freedoms. What did it mean to be faithful? The early Christians hid in caves far from civilization, endured fire, lions, walking on coals and flagellation, things I would have been deadly afraid to do to keep the faith. Never Mary made sure no lost pagan strayed on Sundays. There were times I forgot to follow the script. There I was sitting when I should be standing; my hands dropped to the sides when it should be spread wide, midway through a hug. Or I was staring in another direction when the head should be in direction of the priest. When this happened, Never Mary would appear tapping my shoulder or trying to catch my eye. There were rules to be followed. She was my Lady of Sheshan: the statue of Mary carrying an infant

Jesus while stepping on a red dragon, also called Lady Luck. The lady prevails. She was by the door like a guard dog, not allowing even the curious to wander in, not that she needed to. These people stood out. They stepped in with their eyes thirsty for the spectacle as if the church were an alien spaceship of spires and warmth. Nobody would hurt them here, at worse shoo them away. Some would slip through the net. You could see them imitating the movements of those around them, like keeping time to a beat. They would wet their foreheads from the holy water font or fall in line for communion to stick their tongues out to receive the white circular crisps dipped in sweet consecrated wine. Through it all, she would swoop down to the unsuspecting. She was always there, never merry.

*

What would you believe if you could choose? The government ordered a Day of Silence for those who died in the Sichuan earthquake. It measured eight in magnitude on the Richter scale, killing more than 69,000 people. A three-minute moment of silence would be held in the afternoon at the exact time the ground moved. I wondered what colleagues thought of those who passed away, though I didn't dare ask because couldn't you see it in their faces? Who did they call out? What did they think of death? My faith was tiny, but the thought of oblivion scared me. I visited Sichuan then and remembered how everything numbed the tongue in peppercorns, a spicy and lemony taste. I could not imagine myself cowering under a desk while the ground cracked open and walls crumpled like paper and not call out to a higher being to save me. Chalk it to reasons traced to desperation and deep-seated childhood conditioning. I am a nominal Catholic with doubts. A neighbour went to mass every Sunday only to beat up his children after. Childhood memories of attending mass included me falling asleep in a pew with a dribble of saliva trailing down the side of the mouth. Were they braver and freer for accepting that everything ended at death? And what did it say about myself that I could not let go of being Catholic in a foreign country? This was a place for another version of a life yet there I was recreating homeland habits. Friends considered me odd for how I spent Sundays, a look of incredulity and surprise on their faces. They did not know it was not because of piety that I went. China then until now had the least number of Filipino workers which made encountering one like spotting a rare bird in the wild. When you did hear one, the head craned to the direction of the language like hearing a songbird call out. There were notes of Ilonggo, Waray, Bisaya and Tagalog or was that Bahasa Indonesia I heard? You could not help but stop and listen or follow. Church was nearby based on the number of Filipinos you would bump into headed in the same direction. In winter, I could guess which ones were Filipinos from the back by the thickness and urgency of the fur-lined earmuffs, beanies, scarves and gloves because I was wearing the same. They were like me, people used to tropical living trying vainly to keep warm in negative degree weather. On Sundays, for an hour or so, I was surrounded by the aahhs, naaahhs and infixes that seemed angry and lively to foreign ears but was the rhythm of country to me. I could understand what they were saying. They were thinking of lunch too.

When finally the hour and minute of remembrance for the earthquake came, the whole office stood by the glass walls that looked over the city below. We were on a high floor with a view of the American Race Club clock tower, museum, park and the Samsung signage as prominent as a Hollywood landmark. I said a prayer for those who died, for the one-child children of their one-child parents buried under the rubble of collapsed schoolhouses. I looked far beyond the fringes of the park, squinting at the effort, knowing how we would look like to someone standing outside and looking up: the glass walls reflected the blue sky right back at us as if we were part of the clouds and we'd gone to heaven.

*

You could tell a foreigner had not been in the city long and was on a tight budget by the watering holes they frequented. Not much money and wanting some fun? It was Windows and Zapata's. Windows was popular for university exchange students and those backpacking around Asia on their gap year as English teachers. They lived a more comfortable version of their lives possible only in Asia; a life that could enjoy things otherwise out of reach in their home countries like getting salon sessions before a night out or treating folks to a round of tequila shots. They claimed the right to know and deserve better by the fact that they had the luck to be born in a rich country. They were welcomed because of their passport, and no one questioned why a white man, a white immigrant, would go to Asia, though an Asian would always be treated with suspicion when he made the same journey West, burdened to prove intentions through bank accounts, letters, land titles, tax returns. Were they not the people who brought the evils of colonial oppression and abuse to Asia? It is a class issue that permeates into language and policy when a white person is often referred to as an expatriate while the rest are pigeon-holed with the immigrant, migrant worker label.

I would often see this growing up in Pampanga nearby an American airbase where retired U.S. servicemen complained loudly at restaurants that did not serve hotdogs with real American mustard, or spoke with condescension about facilities in an Asian country, yet were unable to go back home because they could not afford it. Here in Asia, with their citizenship to the country with the strongest military might, their whiteness, their blue eyes, they were somebody when they walked into a bar and everybody knew their name.

For those English teachers, Shanghai was a stop in a world itinerary that included a year or two of travel with breaks at various countries to teach as a way to earn funds for the next journey. Even I went to Windows during the first year of arriving and would stop going, tired of the rowdy crowd. There was always Zapata's. This was the Shanghainese version of a *pueblo* where women drank for free on Margarita Wednesdays. The signage said every day was a party or *cada día es fiesta*. It was a house from the time of the French occupation of the city styled into a watering hole with a large outdoor patio. One hazy memory says I met the owner of Zapata's and contrary to expectations, was a not grizzly bearded man with a potbelly but a petite, sweet-looking woman in furs who was dating an American. The year after it closed down on one winter return, I would stand a few moments outside its unlighted facade still closed and waiting for its next life. I stopped walking, lagging behind friends, mouth agape as if I had seen a shrine, a statue, a monument. The younger self thought this place was great with its cheap alcohol and bawdy fun. Maybe she was right. How could it be here, unexpectedly in front of me after I had written about it? A friend would drag me along not understanding why I would stop and care for some old bar, a place you went to before you knew better. It was cold walking outside, the same unforgiving cold on cobblestoned, tree-lined streets that caused my hand to dry and chap. The same cold that would seep into the rooms. The memory of a shuttered Zapata would be on a loop with a new one: we would continue walking then peek inside the garden of huge house finishing a dinner party with candle lights and flowers on long picnic tables. The owners would see us, chat and invite us in to see the rooms of an art-deco place redesigned with vintage furniture, accessories and sincere, kitschy nostalgia for a Shanghai before everything changed.

But that would happen years and years after I'd left. The morning after a night at Zapata's, I was waking up with a headache and blurry memories that felt enjoyable but didn't make sense. This time around, we were there as part of Johnson's send-off. He was heading back to Beijing then Rome for more books. Pikachu and I would miss our beautiful man of God, worshipped and adored like a saint in our hearts. Tonight we planned to drown our sorrows in margaritas to mourn the loss. He told us he would miss us too, of course, saying it through misty eyes holding our gaze with those long black lashes. I would like to think he kept that gaze only for me.

The crowd began to get noisier as more drinks were passed around by Chinese waitresses dressed like cowboys in shrunken clothes and high boots. People began climbing the lit bar spanning the entire length of the restaurant. Neon lights and loud music went well with the sugary cocktails in huge glasses, its rims dipped in salt. I could barely hear what people were saying as my eyes blinked, hurting from alcohol and smoke. I was drinking much more than I wanted, much more than I promised myself when I arrived in China and vowed to no longer get drunk. The drinks continued to come with only the music being able to talk. Voices began singing loudly in time with stomping feet that formed muddy puddles of spilled drink on the floor.

How many did we drink? Minutes ebbed and flowed. Johnson left our group to head downstairs, where we found him with one hand smoking a cigarette while the other held a drink as his chiselled hips swayed from side-to-side.

He began to unbutton his white shirt while bulges from his arms popped from the effort. I turned to Pikachu and asked if seminarians went to the gym? Johnson had removed more buttons now, his flat stomach visible under dim light. Maybe they did push-ups by the side of the altar, Pikachu told me as her jaw dropped.

Johnson had put down his drink and cigarette and began grinding his ass against a cowgirl emptying a bottle of tequila into his waiting mouth. The last of the buttons revealed an undershirt, so pure, so white. He turned to the woman, holding her close by the hips while torched by light standing on the bar like a deity on a candle-less altar. OMG, we both said. We had never met a seminarian who liked to dance. Then again, didn't holy men dance? Sufi-whirling dervishes spun round and round and round, their skirts floating below their waists like soft white petals buffeted by the wind. Eyes closed, they turned and twirled as meditation, as an offering, in an ecstatic state of ritual, arms in an open embrace to love someone they could not see and never know. I said, were we a bad influence? He seemed to be enjoying himself. She shook her head; it couldn't have been the karaoke nights where we teased him to drink more. Johnson saw us staring and waved. He took off his shirt then as if feeling annoyed by the undershirt and the spotlight, let go of that too. With jeans slung low with a belt, a carved chest glistening in syrupy sweat dripping like ice cream, and eyes closed, Johnson drank from the cup a woman had brought to his mouth until there he was: mainlander, Beijinger, Catholic.

# Inside a Rocking Bus on Tomb-Sweeping Day

When the bus began rocking from side to side, you could feel the bounce of the wheels like being inside a wooden boat on turbulent waves; each sway pushed shoulders further inside the seat now crammed below the bus window. Bus. I knew the word for it: *Gonggong qiche*. The crowd standing outside the bus, their words I could not understand, though they were shouting it in angry huffs, perhaps the language of those who lived around the fields nearby. Why were we all here, cranky and impatient? It was *Qingming* holiday or Tomb-Sweeping Day when a mass exodus ensued of people needing to go home to pay respects to the dead by tidying up tombs and making ritual offerings of joss stick and paper. Imagine a pack of elephants moving across you, when you could hear the rumble even before you turned your head, and maybe you can imagine the hundreds and thousands of people in a hurry to get home on time. It was no surprise then that transport, no matter how adequate and efficient, would be strained or in some places even lacking. People wanted to get out of the nowhere bus station in the middle of somewhere with fields of farmland laid towards a horizon. But, really, why was I here? We were a group of eight people riding the wrong bus; we were riding the wrong bus for an hour. There was no way to get out of the bus. No stop we could get down at but to finish the route and sit, sit, sit. The highways droned on in a straight line, hypnotic, asking you to fall asleep and also ordering one to be patient.

The most fluent Mandarin speakers among us made the mistake of listening to the wrong tones, the pitch, the rising and falling letters, which led to the misinformation. Some of the words did not register in the brain like reading blacked-out text on newspaper but figured, maybe it was in the direction of where we wanted to go, so why not take the chance even if we were not sure. It was near sunset, brushed golden light on golden fields. The surrounding landscape was turning yellow like dyed batik. I looked outside the window to see the set view and let out a sigh, not what I imagined when I agreed to revisit Shanghai after three years. When I was invited to Wenzhou, a place I have never been to, of course, I agreed, like I always did.

First, a statement on the date of the experience. I left in 2010 after almost four years in the mainland and came back in 2013. I expected the view to change from the last time I was there because the person looking at it was not the same as in the process of writing this down now, I am writing about another self. In 2013, I arrived at

Pudong Airport by midnight flight, sleepy yet emotional with nostalgia. The full moon was out and hanging low from the sky; the plane engine rumbled like a monster clearing its throat. From the plane seat, I looked down on a cityscape dotted by yellow lights like acupuncture points marking a body. The plane landed, and more lights blinked in the dark like jewels of citrine, emerald and sapphire. I had forgotten what it felt like to go back to this several times a year.

By the time the seat belts could be safely unbuckled, you struggled out of your seat, to stand, to reach overhead for the hand-carry baggage, to walk to the tube, past the bathrooms, and immigration. There was the grey, more like government office than landing space, bureaucratic efficiency of Pudong Airport. It said its breathy hello with the scent memory of dirty laundry, cigarette smoke and tea, less noticeable than the previous years I lived there. The airport was the same though the rest of China was rapidly changing. I thought maybe something physical had changed; perhaps it was the soap or the spray they used for the airport, but no, it was nothing of that sort. It was me. I was no longer the person holding a tight grip, and a hawk's-eye focus on her luggage. In the early days, I was tense during landing, watched luggage zippers closely, and kept a grim face to look like the sort of traveller you could not fool. The type of person you could not even borrow a pen at the immigration line from, though I looked the opposite. Filipino faces then filled the pages of *Shanghai Daily* because they were caught with drugs in their suitcases, some unsuspecting, some desperate, and paid. These things would happen, yet they say Big Brother was watching everywhere, all the time, filtering, picking up words that criticized the state. One wonders if criticism couched in between words of praise could slip through, or would it have been flagged? People learned to make do with creative and witty ways to slip through search engines and be able to say what they wanted in the symbolic space of the internet that was denied in real life. For example, instead of telling a friend you were going to a rock concert, you would say you were going to school. They used coded terms to signify what they meant while still understood by the rest or flipped images to make it indiscernible to AI.

Big Brother or not, I came prepared with a pen, a digital camera and a handy notebook I could easily take out from the bag without anyone noticing. People asked if I would write about it for a blog or an article. Weepy, I emailed people, friends, ex-boyfriends. I was lamenting on the changing city even before I had stepped out to explore those differences. What was it? Being forced to let go, severing a previous attachment. Freud named it in an essay calling it melancholia for a loss you could not comprehend. The sadness of prior lives. Being there to remember the past was nostalgia, idealized in my head for it meant simpler times when I knew less and wondering what would have happened if I had stayed. I was also a cry baby by nature.

There were notes of places to go, their English and Chinese names jotted down carefully like it was my first arrival. I was looking forward to seeing friends again three years after my exit. Most were still around in the same positions I left them in, but with plans to move back to their countries with anxiety and trepidation or migrate to other places. It was ironic that for Chinese citizens, their freedoms were curtailed by the government, yet for expats away from the prying eyes of family and societal pressure of their culture, they had the privilege of being freer. From being independent, it was back to dependence or a semblance of one when coming back to the familial ties of duty and obligation. The city was a transitional point, a place you passed through because of work, travel and other opportunities but not somewhere you settled in for a lifetime. Many who did stay in China did so moving from one major city to another, their stay contingent on work visas or marrying a Chinese citizen. There were no such things as resident visas or citizenship by place of birth. Chinese friends were migrating to Australia and Canada with families for work and citizenship. Some would move on to postings in other Asian countries. A Chinese friend would ask me to help her fill out immigration forms to leave: the details of a fragmented life distilled in checklists and 'yes' and 'no' questions. For each numbered item, she asked me to explain what it meant. I could understand the desire to leave. She was not the first person I knew who would plot to leave the land of her birth.

\*

Why did I always take red-eye flights? Because I am a cheapskate. I would stay at a friend's apartment this time. Look for it in daylight, and the place was challenging to find within rows of stores and lane houses. Past midnight in chilly weather, it was even harder. The taxis still looked the same; their drivers partitioned away in a resin and metal case, safe from those who would ride his car as if they needed to protect themselves from their customers. In China, it used to be that the customer was always wrong, which changed in less than a decade since I first came. Now, it is, does the customer want soy milk and more snacks along with her hotpot meal? The driver asked for the address.

I had to make do with the Mandarin words and phrases that were returning to me like an amnesia victim being dunked in the water her arms flailing to the sides as she struggled to take in air. The driver pressed on, asking me where I would get dropped off, would he turn left or right? He did not care that I was a foreigner. Speak Mandarin! The words came for the ideas they represented like waves slamming on a shore. Each wave left a coral in its wake, a name, yes! It sounded familiar linked to a memory, a memory signifying an idea and a word. What was it again? I asked myself, feeling the guilt and shame of the slipping knowledge as if they were running away on purpose, giving a chase with me unable to catch them. This language abandonment was the opposite of what I came here for all those years ago. The driver sounded irritated when I paused before answering. Because I was Asian and was often mistaken for being Chinese too, people expected me to be fluent and would laugh or make fun of me when I butchered the words. I tripped on the tones, or they would roll their eyes impatiently when I asked them to repeat what they said, but this time around much, much slower. I was forgetting and had to relearn it on the go, like learning to skate again as you were pushed into the rink. The Mandarin words I knew eroded with time, weathered bit by bit in sediments displaced to a lower slope, another part of my memory and self until the time I need to shake it loose again. But even then, when I was back home, there would be words remembered in Mandarin that would have no meaning in other languages I knew, because they existed in the reality of living in the mainland and could not be found anywhere else. Forgetting then remembering again when back in the environment that taught it to you in the first place felt like your feet never stood on steady ground, that your feet were always kicking, kicking, trying to stay afloat. The methods and strategies to acquire a language are often talked about, but what is equally interesting is why people forget one and what happens then. Does it get triggered when the person is back where she learned it? Does the forgetting begin upon departure? They say people become dormant bilinguals, learning to use one language fluently while the others lie waiting.

The other tricky thing was trying to read the simplified characters again. They had a term to explain when you forgot the characters called *tibiwangzi*. I would see it happen to expats but even locals who, being asked to jot down a Mandarin word by hand, would midway through writing it forget which strokes would come next, then look up to me with a sheepish smile. People were writing less and less with pen and paper and more using computers and phones. It was easier to press keys for the characters to show up on a screen than to write it by hand. Characters were written in strokes by order, yet I wrote them like copying a picture or sketching an object. I once saw a man practising calligraphy in a park, one morning with a bamboo brush dipped in a cup of water. He wrote each character on the black-tiled floor. It was inkless writing, yet the watery characters stood out from the dusty ground. People crowded around him, marvelling at the precise brush strokes.

Children asked to borrow his brush. Was it possible to be alone with language? Sometimes at reunions with friends met in China — those gatherings began to feel like being an alumnus for a chapter of your life you graduated from — after the nostalgia, updates and laughing, one of them would whisper to me to ask: How is your Mandarin? It felt like he was telling me a dirty secret, and in a way, he was. It was a type of failure to forget, and the failure looms larger if you were born into the culture. I did not have Chinese blood, was not born in a Chinese family. His shame was a heavy burden having been born to a traditional family in Manila, been sent to study and live in the mainland several times, and despite it all, even with best efforts, was not able to string two sentences together. He asked me because he knew I was not Chinese and had no burden of kinship for it, unlike whose parents and grandparents spoke it. I could tell from the way he sighed, what he felt was disappointing the legacy by breaking the thread of language that kept them together as a family. I said to myself that not speaking well did not mean I would stop trying on my own.

Armed again with a dictionary, eyes adjusting to the simplified characters now becoming more familiar, I headed downtown to a farewell dinner to meet old friends as well as new ones. There were arrivals to the city, and they had found each other, the newbies and the old-timers by way of connections and referrals. They did not know me but trusted the strength of meeting a friend of a friend of a friend. We had dinner at a Japanese restaurant that cooked dumplings with paper-thin skin stuffed with cheese; delicious, addicting, and small. The farewell party was for a Filipino, leaving for a post in Spain. China was a vast market, so it was no surprise multinational companies expanded there though even a place like Shanghai then was considered a 'hardship' post. Most of those you met were transients to the city to work for a couple of years before being hired for the next job and uprooting themselves again.

I stuck out in these circles because there were simply less media companies for foreign workers in the city; the only writer in a roomful of people working in manufacturing and marketing selling shampoo and soap to the huge Asian market. Most of the media companies chose to open in Beijing, thus most of the writers were there. Even then, saying that seems inaccurate. I have always found myself in groups where I don't quite fit in which made people scratch their heads when they meet me. A part of me wishes I had conformed more to society's rules and expectations on what a good life should look like on paper then, again, where was the imagination in that?

If you've been around in Shanghai long enough, farewell parties become commonplace and heart-breaking. A decades-long China expat told me about how she stopped making friends with he ones she knew would leave after a few years, tired of showing the ropes to those who would surely not be there after. It hurt too much to care, then say goodbye, she said. She made friends with people who were permanently living there like her, otherwise it felt like circling the same tracks, returning to the starting point then getting back to a life you once left. In Shanghai, people knew they would not stay long so there was always the dread of coming home and re-entering a life you turned your back from. It is hard to say goodbye to people when you've made space for them to occupy in your routine. It was also, in a way, a symbiotic relationship like those seen in the wild where a small creature will tag along with another one as they glide on the ocean floor in search of adventure. A newly arrived expat living in a country with a difficult language to learn will need another expat in their lives with better fluency to help them.

Sometimes what I can remember are memories of memories that seemed to have all happened in one day. Again the meeting with former colleagues as they treated me out to lunch felt good and it was great to see them, though we all knew this would be the last time.

People were unhappy at work and were making other plans. The office was moving to a smaller one, another building with more competition from overseas coming in. People asked me why I had left then returned, asking with nervousness how it would feel to go back. I went back because of family and wanting to build something. Was there anything to go back to? It had taken courage to leave, it was courage again to return and leave behind the life you built. How do you keep friendships you've made long after you have gone? There are no straight answers to that other than you try your best and show up. In the expat life, the names overlap and connect like links to a tangled chain. You hear a person's name, like hearing sounds from distant waves repeated because you move in the same group. The stories are shared, and connections resurface. Friendships that grew under these conditions became harder to keep because of its dependence on place and atrophied social ties from home that made it possible to accept new people in life.

*

I wanted to take the five days for a pilgrimage of my old life. Things did not go as planned. Because it was an extended holiday, friends decided to take a nearby trip to Zhejiang and asked if I wanted to come along. It was a surprise to me because I wanted to stay in Shanghai and visit haunts that I miss. That was not meant to be, I suppose. I had different ideas for a return trip back to the city. What was a planned five-day tour, was scrapped for two days because though I wanted to go around on my own, I also wanted company. The past version of myself was afraid to be alone. I ended up having two days for myself to trace the steps of a past life like watching a movie unspool to the beginning of the reel. I would wake up in a rush to get to work in the subway behind our flat, yet even the view was not the same anymore. There were more subway lines than I could remember. The block of lane houses I used to see outside my room window decorated by flags of drying laundry and criss-crossed wires was replaced by a parking lot. The walk to the subway now more glaring with the coloured light of advertisements on the wall moving with you like scenes from a science-fiction movie.

\*

Pikachu still hadn't left, she is a manager now, but this time instead of Filipino roommates, she was living with French girls she met through Craigslist. I stayed at her place for a day in Shanghai, in her roommate's coat-crammed room, before we were off to Zhejiang. A few hours away from Shanghai, Zhejiang was cold though it was blue sky. What were we doing here at the Yunhe Terraces when we had terraces of our own back in the Philippine archipelago? We went to Yunhe Terraces and Lishui Lake, where what we thought was a failure for the day ended up looking like a cut scene from an Ang Lee film. The lake was still as heavy fog descended at sunset. There was nothing to see so tourists had gone and we were alone staring at the ghostly white layer. For a moment though, the cloudy fog lifted slowly like curtains coming up on a theatre stage and a lone dark figure with a conical hat and a steering pole in his hands drifted in on a bamboo raft. We all scrambled to take a photo, the desire to capture the moment greater than the need to be in the moment, when if we stopped to take in, it was like being inside a fable.

*

Back to the bus, the setting sun drew line marks through the window. It rattled on and on; we didn't know where we were going only that the road rolled for miles into a dot ahead of us. By the time we stopped, it was confirmed: we were at the wrong stop in the middle of nowhere. The day had turned out both long and short at the same time. It was pointless to blame someone for misunderstanding a language he wasn't a master of, of the task of keeping two or three languages churning inside your head, each one interrupting the other. So now here we were in the middle of a mad crowd. It was the holidays when people went back to their hometowns in droves to visit their dead relatives. There was a desperate rush to leave. An angry crowd gathered around us, demanding to be let on the bus. They began rocking it from side to side: sway, sway, sway. Not content, people began climbing through the open windows as the shouts became louder. I could feel my hands starting to sweat and jaw tense up from fear. Cases of mob violence were something that I read about often

in the news but never witnessed in the country until then.
The anger spread in the crowd like a priest anointing people
with holy water. I wondered how we would be able to leave.
Some of us were scared because we were the lone foreigners
in the bus. If people knew we did not need to take that bus
ride to make it in time for an important family occasion
such as they did, who knows what they would have done to
us? I never saw Pai look as pale as he did back then, his face
turning to an even sickly shade of white. He was the only
guy in the group. He signalled to our other companions to
stop talking. They didn't and continued to chat not paying
attention to the upset crowd.

The sun markings inside the bus were blocked by
people now; people climbing through open windows. At
the back, a man screamed at someone crawling to get inside.
He said something before shutting the windows close.
I looked down at my fingers, careful to keep the face blank.
Someone might hear we were not locals as I shut my mouth.
If they found out, there would be mayhem, a lot of pushing
and shouting until someone bled red and left. Reports of
mangled bodies due to crowd hysteria were common items
in the news. What did trampled bodies stepped on by feet
and pushed by uncaring hands look like? Like chopped
up chicken or meat, soft and bruised by neglect. This we
knew, but the rest of us did not. They continued to talk
in English and even began talking louder so they could
hear themselves speak. Would arms pop out of the window
beside her and drag her out as if in a zombie apocalypse?
I imagined my face bruised and eyeglasses broken into two.

Finally, after a lot of white-knuckle clutching on the pleather bus seats, the bus was able to wiggle off the crowd clinging to its shell like a tortoise shaking off parasites. Yet, some remained tenacious. The bus was able to move at last when the driver floored the gas pedal stronger this time, to take us out of there and leave the yellow fields welcoming spring.

It was a wasted day, but among wasted days, it was the most memorable, like pocketing crystal from a trash heap. I was on an enjoyable trip trading jokes and quips with a group of Filipino expats new to the city. We had flown into Wenzhou together while another friend was inevitably left behind when he wasn't able to wake up on time. We went back and retraced our route, scratching our heads, wondering what we were doing there in the first place, in this place, a couple of hours' drive from Shanghai to see, of all things — rice terraces when we were from a country whose major livelihood was planting rice, a country where you could eat rice for breakfast, snacks, lunch and dinner. We looked happy in the photos though more for the relief of having made it this far than the actual sight of it. I remembered my rubber shoes sank on the soft soil still wet from being planted by rice stalks as we took turns to have photos among the terraces.

We huddled in a circle to plot the next day's schedule. In our group, almost all spoke Mandarin, but only two spoke it fluently enough that they were depended on to make the arrangements, book the tour. Wenzhou City in Zhejiang was known for having the greatest number of self-made millionaires and yet not much else. The parks were picturesque, clean and, surprisingly, empty of crowds. We had the place to ourselves. I have a photo of standing on a rock while a stream flowed around me. While riding on a cramped cab we haggled with to get the prices down and on our way to the park, we were finally excited. A mountain slope was covered in leaning willow trees, graceful and soft like hair swept by the wind. We stopped by the side of the road to marvel at the serene swaying forests. Even the driver could not help but smile at our enthusiasm while only moments ago we could barely understand each other. The season undressed colours, turning to the glow of the sun.

# BEIJING

# Days and Nights in Magic Land

There was a chance to revisit Beijing, but this time with friends from work. It would be different from the first time I went during winter when our skin shrivelled, and peeled from the dry cold. Memories of the city were a mist, like the wispy branches found in calligraphy paintings, we walked across from one chilly end of the Forbidden City to the other without pause. A conscripted version of Beijing through the window of a bus before it was back to the budget hotel and the flight back. Accommodations for this trip was a flat borrowed from a friend living in the central district who was away for business. Spacious bachelor living had an air of abandonment with its pack of moulded cheese bitten off in the fridge and tables littered with bottles of beer and vodka. It was no better than a hotel, at least that had room service. The day was a bruised sky when we arrived like the rest of the days that would follow in this city built on a desert with roads so broad; a fairy-tale giant could lie down flat and still have room to wiggle his arms.

Chaoyang district was dull-coloured on those days like laundry wash; its buildings indistinguishable from each other back then, unlike the extroverted buildings of Shanghai. Though in some parts, it seemed like it took a page from a speculative-fiction story like the grey building with a missing centre standing like a drawn square or one with a chiselled facade like a mountain, except it was fabricated. You travel to see places that have withstood time, or lives continually in the present. Here it felt neither the present nor the past but the next thing still making up its mind. The city kept the glory of its Communist past and the Soviet idea of urbanity with standard and simplified lines. The smog did nothing for the view making the capital seem hooded and sleepy though I don't remember needing a face mask or did we stay in then, saved by filters and windows sealed in shut? Air quality was life quality that made jokes about living in the city, dystopic and absurd. A company sold hand-bottled air from the Canadian Rockies, while another gave away canned air as social satire lost on me until explained.

The trip was with colleagues who had become friends: Snap, Waverly and Pat. I was one of the few foreigners and the only Filipino who worked as an editor in a publishing company that helped capitalists enter the Chinese market. The company held the hand of nervous investors wanting to do business in China but didn't know where to start. At the flat, Snap opened the curtains letting the light in and with it the longing for her 20s. She was Shanghainese who lived in Beijing for five years. It was here that she would find work as a photographer before going into graphic design.

In her photos, people stood in singles: a child on the move in a padded velvet seat theatre for hundreds; a dying rose in a lush field or a suited man with eyes closed and hands spread downwards in a park. Was that how she saw the world? She was a woman late in the years with no boyfriend and uninterested in marriage. There is a term used to refer to a single, well-educated, successful woman called *sheng nu* or leftover girl. In the Philippines, the term used for unmarried women was old maid. Like my family, her parents didn't seem to mind if she was leftover, only thing that mattered was that she was their daughter. They lovingly packed her lunch each working day as they did since she was a child. She spoke with fondness of the weekends spent exploring Beijing highways that stretched out to the countryside by car. On these road expeditions, she would take more photos until the film rolls stacked on her feet. They did not want to save for property; they wanted to see the world. Driving was still new to her generation, even the thought, no, the act of buying and owning a car was a novelty, she said. I nodded, understanding. I used to brace myself not to act in panic when Waverly offered to take me home, having learned to drive a car recently. She drove the vehicle as if she were still riding a motorbike swerving in and out of traffic quickly, suddenly stepping on the brakes and speeding. Waverly was there because she did not want to miss out. I teased her for not having visited the capital sooner. The centre of six dynasties, I said. She rolled her eyes, saying there was nothing exceptional about a wall, and so what of the feudal lords of kingdoms. The rivalry between Shanghai and Beijing was a source of amusement when it came time to talk to people from both cities. Beijingers told me the Shanghainese were materialistic and money-minded, looking over their shoulders waiting for me to agree while the Shanghainese criticized Beijingers for uncouth manners and backwardness. They prided themselves for their Western sophistication. To me, their similarities were more than their differences. Waverly's mother would visit us from Guangzhou, then afterward, she would admit to enjoying the city. She was not what I would hear people there refer to as — often with condescension or pity — migrant farmer stock, the ones who flocked big cities for better jobs and lost their social benefits due to the *hukou* system. *Hukuo* was the household registration limiting where you could live and avail government services. She studied and worked in Copenhagen before coming back to Shanghai for good.

Her family's rising fortunes swam with the waves sweeping the rest of the country, changes that came after less than a generation when her parents began from being assembly workers in a car factory in Guangzhou to opening their own business. During those early years, her father lined up before dawn, clutching a coupon allowing him to buy the family's first electronic appliance. Pat, on the other hand, was a Thai-Indian, who carried a Thai passport but grew up in New Delhi, then studied in Scotland. The only phrase she could say in Thai was: I don't speak Thai. She had the annoying habit of correcting me to follow British English pronunciation, which was strange because

I was Filipino. I never lived in England either. Speaking with a British accent would make me seem pretentious and insufferable.

Our first stop in Beijing was Simatai. A part of the Great Wall farther out from the city, a two-hour drive to be exact, compared to the nearer Badaling. Simatai was better for its expanse of the wall; the stones had not given way, and visitors were fewer, although there were travellers everywhere, including ourselves. Tourists hate other tourists the most when they are there for the same thing: to experience the real, the local. It was for the hope that authenticity was possible, and encountering it would imbibe us with a unique point-of-view because of the effort and expense it took to get there. At the wall, time unrolled like a dense carpet. Feet turned leaden from the weight of what we knew. We knew the wall would march on. Walking the whole length of 5,000 miles would take eighteen months. What lay beyond the wall when it could survive even an era without men? I liked the idea of culture outliving me like the tortoise. The Great Wall was so magnificent that it seemed like it was conjured from thin air, magicked with enchanted dust not made with the passing of a thousand years. Didn't David Copperfield walk through it? Frustration, fear, anger, life could melt away, and bombs could fall from the sky, yet the wall would remain here. The wall probably wished it could run away from us — the annoying sightseers that would disturb its peace during daytime and at nighttime keep it awake with rave parties. Its reason for being was to keep the northern barbarians out, but now the barbarians were not only inside but on top of it, and they paid to get there. The enemy made hotels, pilfered it for bricks and dirtied its face with spray paint. The misconception was, it was visible from outer space when evidence said it was not. From this grounded version of a wall, a virtual one was built, the Great Firewall of China to block internet access and watch over each citizen's use of it. A virtual net strung as high as the real Great Wall to bounce off unsavoury keywords though even then like the actual wall, it was not impermeable to a witty analogy or catchy homophones, like a spear thrown over the wall, whizzing and gaining momentum.

It took us an hour of climbing before we reached a beacon tower where we could rest and see the landscape beyond the fence. We sweated under the summer heat. Why did I pay good money to get here? Travel must be half suffering with the rest of it reserved for the grit of being born with a third world passport for the chance to move from one point to another. You are left with a bag of ten per cent, maybe less, to pin your pleasure on. Could it be that what a real vacation was — staying in a room doing nothing away from everything? I asked myself why I wanted to climb up the longest wall in the world.

Other tourists were there to have their photos taken by the windows with their back against the winding stairs. This section was said to have been built in the fifth century and again in the 15th century. The climb to the beacon tower became steeper as we hugged the stones and lowered our bodies to the ground so as not to topple over. Over my shoulder, I could see other people do it as if they were strolling in a park. Some parts of the wall were more extensive while some narrower. I grabbed as much of it as I could. Unfortunately, I was climbing the Great Wall, not wearing great shoes.

On my feet were thin-soled rubber shoes, which let me feel every nook and cranny. Reflexology points were massaged. I could have lost a kidney. They say there is a section of the wall where each stone is marked with the maker's name and date. These were not those stones. They were anonymous as those who built them centuries ago and the ones that would walk their paths centuries after. As visitors were on their way up, the others were on their way down. We saw their backs as they walked past us in the middle of the Great Wall. The rhythm of the crowd was a consolation. It was a promise you could climb this ridiculous length and not only survive but go back. We were thrilled to be there to see a glimpse of what we could touch with our hands before us yet never see in its entirety in this lifetime or the next. Even here, money was pegged and made. Vendors were selling dried fruit and t-shirts. A cable car ready for those not wanting to climb. On one part of the wall, we rode a zip line to reach the other end. In a photo, I am standing with a nervous smile, a green shirt crumpled by a harness. By then, my mind began to tire of thinking of barriers and dividers that a wall seemed to form in my thoughts — a walled resistance?

The next day, we went to the Forbidden City with Snap's old friend, Dove, who also gave us a history lesson while acting as a guide. The Imperial Palace is the top draw in Beijing for having the best name suited for a tourist attraction: Forbidden City. How could you not go when the name says you shouldn't? Commerce was not forbidden, though. In 2007, a Starbucks would open inside its hundred-year-old walls serving tall, grande and venti from the former seat and home of 24 emperors. It was packed with people when I went, but now the Starbucks was gone. The structures were freshly painted of what they called *gugong red*, a temple red used for landmarks in China. The bright, slick, shiny newness reminded me of a theme park as it did for revolution and luck. The red colour was combined with shades of green and blue with images of the dragon and the phoenix, considered auspicious symbols of the emperor. It was the same red used for money envelopes with gold-embossed letters. She brought us around the rooms and across the compound for the impossible task of compressing half a century's worth of history in a few hours. Dove brought us to the throne room where the cunning Empress Dowager Cixi ruled China during the Qing dynasty. Dove's faithful retelling of court politics and gossip left me with a headache. I could not remember half the names she mentioned. The stories did not seem to follow a straight line but meander, go back and start over again.

Of the rooms in the Forbidden City, it was the bathroom that concerned me the most, where it was, and how to get there. How many Heavenly Gates and Halls of Supreme Harmony did I need to cross to reach it? Did they have squat toilets or not? The squat toilet was a precarious position to be in; it meant you had no problems with your knees and could bend your legs comfortably, not to mention the risk of slipping while on the way up or falling on your back. Wasn't it squatting that one did before jumping over a ditch? Dove was annoyed at my question, having disturbed her long speech about the imperial symbolism found in the palace. Waverly laughed. Talk shifted to the woman who worked in our Beijing office, who was a relative of the last emperor, Pu Yi, maybe a great cousin or a niece. A photo of her showed a woman in a coat with cropped hair, bangs and eyeglasses during a company outing. They were excited to have her around. Royalty can look banal; I could have passed her on the street. Now she was working as an accountant in Beijing, helping foreigners invest in China. I pictured how their family must have survived communism, given who they were, to live life as citizens outside the walls. Perhaps anonymity was a relief, an undressing, to be stripped of the past and begin again. Loss of identity meant freedom from persecution during revolutionary times and no more expectations. This loss was a price to pay for the chance to live freely as the last of the Manchus. We marvelled that we were in the palace she would have stayed in if the empire endured. Our heads likely decapitated as punishment for the crime of entering. What if I were a man in that lifetime? I could have been a low-ranked mandarin with shaky calligraphy barely entering the ranks. She would be wearing a robe of intricate embroidery; her thoughts weighed down by a headdress of flowers and beads. Would she wonder about another life lived as she spent days painting and embroidering while pampered by servants and wrapped in silk? To make the possibility of another kind of life possible, a kingdom she knew had to end.

As we went around, Pat looked unimpressed. We stared blankly at the pieces of encased broken glass, a jade comb and a mirror in one of the rooms. The remaining furniture inside the rooms was placed against the wall or in the centre like a ceremonial offering. These were the strange glamour of those years when the cows were fat before they were abandoned, as if waiting for ghosts to return. She asked, where are the jewels? The gathered treasures of the centuries? She told me of Mughal emperors with palaces embedded with emeralds. Waverly was beginning to look bored. I was also expecting objects of wealth, of porcelain, jade, gold and glittering stones. These treasures we were looking for turned out to be in the Palace Museum located on the same grounds and the National Palace Museum in Taipei.

Snap would take us to have a photo in front of Zhongnanhai next, the seat of government. You passed by a white stone bridge to reach the southern gate with a red wall and a building with peaked rooftops. There were gigantic red lanterns strung on the ceiling, and Mao Zedong's portrait hung over the main entrance with two slogans, also red. Waverly said the slogans went, long live the great CCP and long live the strong Mao Zedong's beliefs. Journalists often referred to it as the walled heart of the Chinese Communist Party. Zhou Enlai passed through these gates on the grounds of a former garden built by the emperor. This complex was China's real Forbidden City because you could not go in.

As for me, the word Zhongnanhai meant a brand of cheap cigarettes sold on the streets. Lighting up a stick of Zhongnanhai, in translation both meant smoking up China's Kremlin and Central and Southern Seas. It also meant that I would cough and wheeze from the incessant second-hand smoke indoors because I was also in a way smoking China's Kremlin, its Central and Southern Seas. The name was also one of the singles from the band Carsick Cars' first album which became an anthem for the Beijing indie music scene with catchy riffs and clangy guitars sequence with the words:

*Zhongnanhai, Zhongnanhai,*
*Zhongnanhai, Zhongnanhai*

I was there the same year that Chinese indie rock bands were releasing albums in what they would call a rock revival. I watched Carsick Cars live in Shanghai at an underground club, which meant making the trip to a converted building far from the city. A friend had told me about the band, saying we had to go to their concerts to hear them. The albums were not in shops, nor their music played on the radio. Rock music had been banned since the 1990s because of the Tiananmen massacres, which were used to fuel the protests. To release an album, state censors required musicians to submit the lyrics of their songs. One had to go to the source. Sadly, in our office khakis and loafers, we could not pass for college kids and were charged full admission price. In the next life, maybe I will have the talent to sing and perform. It was not unusual after knowing I was Filipino to be asked next if I could sing a song or dance, more so in Shanghai where Filipinos have been singing professionally. Lee William Atkins, in his paper, mentions Filipinos who joined the Shanghai band scene along with Russian migrant musicians in 1881, although they would leave and move to Hongkong with the Chinese Revolution of 1949. They played *shi dai qu* or fashionable songs learned from the Americans back home, filling the poshest venues at hotels.

Oh to be young! The place was full, red and blue light filled the small stage as we waited for them to appear. There was a bar for drinks while standing around. Carsick Cars was three scrawny guys on a stage playing stripped-down, bare guitar punk music. Heads bobbed to the live rhythm, and people began jumping. They knew the songs. I straightened and bent my knees up and down to go with the movement, careful not to spill the overpriced cocktail. There was no way to tell each band member apart because of the lights and their uniform appearance. The sound was a surprise to me, which up until then only heard sticky-sweet Cantopop music and ballads in Mandarin while in the mainland. The music was familiar though because it was an homage to Sonic Youth, though by the act of translating it in Mandarin Chinese on that stage in the 2000s in Communist China it was already different and not an uncanny mimic of an American band. In the book, *Red Rock: The Long Strange March of Chinese Rock & Roll*, Jonathan Campbell calls the music *yaogun* as specific to Chinese rock and roll. It was unavoidable that as I listened to the lyrics, I looked for hidden meanings or hints of dissent knowing the band came from Beijing. I was politicizing their work because of the context of where they lived. I listened to their song about picking brightly coloured mushrooms that turned into red mushrooms in the village then being caught by police. Maybe it was about drugs? What if counter-culture for them was being apolitical? What if they wanted to play music, be famous and not change the world? Punk rock traces its roots to rejection and rebellion of mainstream culture. The straightforward response would be to presume they were making freedom rock. What if it annoyed them that people heard them for their perceived biases against the country and not for the lyrics or the music itself?

We walked across Tiananmen Square quietly without comment after Zhongnanhai. I was waiting for Dove to say something, anything really, but we ended taking more photos. It was my second time there and also the second time a Chinese person crossed with me on Tiananmen Square during a tour without telling me what happened on the fourth of June in 1989 when thousands of protesters were killed. Maybe she did not have a reason to say anything to me, a foreigner, of what happened there since it was something she barely remembered herself. During the Tiananmen Square demonstrations, rock music became the student anthem. The song was *Nothing to My Name* by Cui Jian, considered the father of Chinese rock. The album cover was the singer wearing a red blindfold.

He sang the words of a man asking a woman to go with him even though he had nothing: '*I want to give you my hope/I want to help make you free/But you always laugh at me/ For I have nothing to my name*'. Where was I in 1989?

I was not yet a teen, playing games in the afternoons and flying kites made of bamboo sticks, Japanese paper and rice glue. The memory of the event came from scenes watched on the television, while I sat with legs folded on the floor in between episodes of a telenovela soap. Four tanks rolled into a square, and a man in a white long-sleeved shirt stood in front of them. They called him Tank Man. There was also the memory of a dense crowd carrying large red flags that you could no longer see the floor where they stood. I sat there not understanding what was happening but knowing enough to be able to tell it was terrible. This was mixed with memories of the 1980s, of a dead body in white laying face down on a tarmac and nuns with flowers during the People Power Revolution.

My parents didn't talk to me. I knew the grown-ups were upset. Relatives had joined the protests. The environment and socially conscious pop group, Smokey Mountain, then ahead of its time, was playing on the radio, and their song, *Paraiso*, was a hit. The Americans still kept their biggest airbase in Asia in the Philippines. I played with the military kids, trying to imitate the slang words they used when they spoke, but would soon forget. Early mornings on the street were sometimes noisy, as I heard an American shouting and cursing his wife with loud banging and more shouting then, later on, in a fit of repentance, make a show of cooking for her in the yard. The swing across our house was always full of neighbourhood kids waiting for their turn. An uncle went to China after opening reforms, travelling all over the country in trains with a group of friends. They were guided by an activist who was stranded in the country after Martial Law and now spoke fluent Mandarin. He said they ate the food of emperors or at least he was told that. What else was there? The pop group, Wham overtook Queen and the Rolling Stones to become the first Western band to play in China after it opened the country to trade. It would play its songs about waking up before you go, go in Beijing in front of 12,000 bewildered people still wearing Cultural Revolution-style clothes of blue, green and grey. Even before Wham came to China, another foreign band supposedly would play before them according to Campbell, a Filipino surf-pop group called Nitaige'er who came in 1982.

After Zhongnanhai, the next stop was an art street near the palace. Here, memories fail me. I would forget the name of the street except for its wide road with rows of coffee, art and craft shops, which describes a lot of the city's mazes. We wandered the small shops tucked within alleys, their grey brick walls and peaked tile roofs slung low. They were one-floor dwellings compared to two or three-floor ones in Shanghai. On climbing the top of one, I saw a sea of rooftops spanning far and wide, each one so close to each other as if touching tip to tip. I could picture myself jumping out of that terrace and hopping from one rooftop to another as if catching ripples until I was no more than a speck from a distance, off, off to be forgotten; lost among the views. The trees with twisty branches would wave me away, but I didn't, only ended up taking a photo, turning my back at the sight to climb down the steep stairs to join friends below.

The stores were staffed by the artists who made their wares by hand. Waverly and Pat bought canvas tote bags with Communist slogans done in pop-art style. What was once a revolution and communist object had become a tourist trinket, to be ditched and forgotten like paper tickets when you get back home after weeks on the road. Snap dragged me to have coffee with her friend from Peking University. A moon gate that pointed to more moon gates opened until it ended into a courtyard garden where we would sit. I was thrilled to meet someone studying robotics in Peking and looked at her like one would stare at a unicorn, imagining how she was able to breathe in that rarefied air where competition to get in must have been cutthroat. To get in the best university in a country of one billion people, she had to outrank the estimated nine million applicants who took the national entrance exams or the *gaoke* every year. I half expected her to be speaking in some ancient language like Sumerian.

The whole street was noisy, with people drinking coffee, tea, and talking. The afternoon light was fading at its edges like a tea stain. I wish I could have sat there for long, melted into the chair seat until my face was a blob wearing an expression of contentedness. Pat asked again if we could eat roast duck for dinner. I wondered then as I sat there with them, these people I met in Shanghai, who

I would have been if I decided to go to Beijing instead? The choice of a city was a refusal of the other possibilities where I could have also built a life. Would I have been the same person? And if I ask that then I also ask what if I was born in another country instead of the Philippines, would life have been better? People I had met who lived in Beijing first lament how the experience was better in the capital: friends were closer, the nights were longer. They told me expats in Beijing were friendlier. Timing had a lot to do with that brand of happiness. They arrived and knew Beijing first; by the time they moved to Shanghai, things had lost the shine of novelty. It was more of the same old, same old in a different place.

I say this because it was the opposite for me. I went to Beijing, comparing it to Shanghai like pitting one suitor against another. In 2008, Beijing would host the Olympics and, with it, spend close to US$40 billion worth of infrastructure to organize it. Tickets would become a competitive sport in itself. The Olympic Green was through Subway Line 8, named Aolin Pike Gongyuan, a phonetic equivalent of the word, Olympic Park. Spanning more than a thousand hectares of space, touring the grounds felt like roaming a forest. We would see the Beijing National Stadium, which was called the Bird's Nest because of the twisted steel beams that did make it look like its name, although if not told and hungry, I could also have said it was a squished taro ball.

There was a running litany of complaints about the trip: the weather was worse in the capital; the streets composed of many lanes exhausting to cross; the subway too old; the city too large. It felt like one needed a helicopter or plane to pass one part of the city to another. Legs were never long enough to cover the miles that had no end, the avenues that were six lanes wide. The gap between points grew longer as if conjured; from the Great Wall it became the Great Walk Around Beijing.

The duck dinner that Pat pined about would be at a hidden courtyard among a maze of alleys where they cooked it the old-fashioned way. It was such a top secret that there was a welcome sign for tourists painted on the entrance wall. The restaurant was at a back-alley with dubious sanitation standards the mind ignored on purpose and a good measure of red and gold lanterns. We were one of the many foreigners there. I behaved like a proper visitor should by taking photos, marvelling at the brick kiln where fire licked the ducks hanging inside. The uncooked ducks were hung in a line, their long necks tucked in like folded paper while their bodies shone yellowish skin glowing like aged *mahjong* tiles. Men in uniforms brought each duck inside an open brick oven where it could rest and languish as if in a spa. After each session, the ducks were hung like laundry on hooks posted on a white tile wall now yellow from the years. The night would be remembered with a smile, having drunk as much *Tsingtao* beer and ate as much duck as we could. Waverly's mother sliced the special mooncakes with double egg yolk brought from Guangdong for good luck. Then the years after that moment would pass, and I would leave China, and so would they. Snap to the

United States, Pat to England, and Waverly to Australia. The last time I would talk to Waverly was while riding her red sports car. She had traded up, from driving a mini car that barely fit a suitcase to one that cost as much as a house. The family became richer. Her looks also changed; she lost the baby fat and wore so many logos on her person it was distracting.

Oh, but that night, that night inside a *hutong*, I remember. The lazy susan groaned from the weight of the food, although everything would pale in comparison to the duck. The duck skin cracked like an ice shard when cut and had a layer of jiggly gelatinous fat that disappeared on the tongue. The crispy skin was lacquered shiny red like the Ming Dynasty-style chairs we sat on with their high backs and knobs curling upwards. These were the memories of us spending days and nights in magic land, a city I would never understand like my own archipelagic heart. I wish I knew then that trip would be our last one together before we went our separate ways, but I acted like it was any other trip because it was.

# LHASA

# We Go to the Land of Snow

Before going, what I knew of the words 'Shangri-La' was as a hotel and a shopping mall famous in Asia. It would be later that I would make the connection to the place written about in stories. I told Kevin my excitement for the big trip to Lhasa in Tibet. It was a last hurrah of sorts since the visa would expire soon, time in Shanghai was an upturned timer with the sand sucking to its end fast. Jobs were hard to come by, and each rejection became more depressing than the last. I had gotten it into my head that a trip to Tibet would be a fitting close. This was what I told Kevin, who, true to past behaviour and sombre self, replied to me with a *chengyu*, an idiom: *ban tu er fei*. Pfft, the little fuck. He was doing it again, showing off his encyclopedic memory of *chengyus* pulled from a Chinatown childhood spent watching television. He knew I would not understand what he said but would know enough to perceive that he was asserting his intellectual superiority by not giving a straight answer. Replying using classical idioms made him appear highly educated and obtuse. So I had to ask:

> What does it mean?
> To give up when you're halfway there.
> And?
> It is deep, don't you think? Keep that in mind when you travel to Tibet.

Kevin was uninterested in goodbyes. He could not wait to leave and vowed never to come back because of a mainland he hated for a vastly different reason: people treated him like a local. He fought for the right to be called a Filipino, a label wrangled with strangers to bequeath him. This rejection and refusal caused conflict wherever he went as he fought for his identity at shops, on the subway, inside the campus, and at our favourite neighbourhood noodle place. It would begin with an innocent question of where he was from then change to disbelief until it blew up into bitter arguments with raised voices and fists. When this happened, Medal and I would begin looking at our feet or the crowd around us to avoid being caught in the argument. He fought his detractors in pitch-perfect Mandarin. What they said was true, though to admit it in front of him, would be a betrayal of our new friendship still under probation. It would be the first time I would hear the pejorative Hokkien term, *tai diok ka* or TDK used to refer to Chinese newcomers to the Philippines. Medal to his credit never used it to refer to Kevin only to show his stricken face at the mounting realization that not only was Kevin fresh off the boat but that his ship never left the shore. The same thing happened when he went to Beijing, where he was furious for being prevented from entering a foreign student's residence because they did not believe he was an international student. He would lose a tooth later on during a drunken brawl in the city's Houhai Lake where he drowned frustration with cheap alcohol. One night on the way home, a Uighur teen whose father sold grilled lamb skewers near where we lived began following us wanting to know about the Philippines and taking his chance to talk to foreigners who spoke Mandarin. He pointed to us then to Kevin, adding he was a mainlander, a *zhong guo ren*. We could not blame him because even we could see it, but we had to stifle giggles and come to his defence. Despite having lived in Manila all his life and speaking fluent Tagalog, Kevin was more Chinese in looks, clothing and behaviour than anyone we knew. He was like a plant grafted to foreign soil that continued to grow the same way despite the change in terrain. It was a puzzle why he was studying Mandarin when his speaking was better than excellent — it was native. In a Chinese school in downtown Manila, he was teased as China Man. He lived in an alternate Manila I did not know when he admitted to not knowing the Philippines was colonized by the Spaniards. When? He asked me, genuinely shocked. There is also a *chengyu* for that too: *bu ke si yi* or unbelievable.

I had gotten it in my head to travel to Tibet because it was a mysterious place, hard to get into because of political reasons. An uncle tried to enter once when the riots began after journeying to the place where Confucius was born. The younger self wanted bragging rights. I had stopped drinking then, reformed my ways. Tibet was a dream destination even though I didn't know what the dream was, to begin with. I wanted to go because it was a forbidden, religious place and, other than Pikachu, a friend who would go with Italians, I never knew anyone else who went. Pikachu said to eat chocolate before ascent. The trip was my idea, and three other Filipinos were joining me: Medal, Box and Prof. They latched on to my enthusiasm, which was all there was, I did not know how to get there. If I had known more before we left, I would never have done it. We knew no one and could not afford a guided tour. We would do the travel arrangements ourselves and book everything as we went along. An itinerary was drawn as we moved from one place to another.

This was how I found myself sitting on a train window watching the snow-wrapped landscape and lakes go by for hours and hours on the way to Tibet. I sat on a folding chair beside a wide window with yellow curtains pulled back. There was a strip of what was intended to be a table enough for instant noodles and a bottle of tea. We had left Chengdu and before that Xi'an to see the faded glory of the Terracotta Army, the pottery avatars of a once real one, resplendent, at some point, in black, pink, purple, green and reds, the pigments had disappeared with exposure. They were brown now and cordoned off at the pit where they were discovered. Even the chariot with horses meant to carry the emperor to life after death was there. A friend recalled the time when she had been allowed inside the pit, and seeing my surprised face, she added: we were allowed to touch them.

For some of the sites, it was the stuff of the absurd. One park had us climb what felt like hundreds of steps up to Mount Li and pay a hefty fee to see the burial ground of the first emperor of China who wanted to live forever — Qin Shi Huang. At the end of that long climb was a stone marker saying we must imagine how the burial chambers must look like because no one has seen it. The emperor did not find the elixir to immortal life but lives now through the fame of the funerary art he commissioned. Imagine working for a boss like that, someone who wants you there during the after hours and the afterlife. The chambers remained unopened in what they claim were one hundred rivers of mercury underneath us, according to ancient lore. This was information I wish we had known before heaving and panting through the climb up the mountain.

Medal acted the enthusiastic tour guide as he regaled me with the story of the Romance of the Three Kingdoms, his favourite growing up, and the brave and fair ruler, Zhuge Liang, which made the museum stops interesting. I knew nothing about the historical novel, *Sanguozhi*, before the trip. Medal painted the complicated, mythical plot for me in broad strokes, a saga of 120 chapters to rival even the most complicated of fantasy novels. At the Xi'an Museum, sculptures of full-figured women were displayed in various states of repose. During the Tang Dynasty, to be fat was to be rich. It meant you could afford to eat well.

To be slim and skinny meant the opposite. I looked at those women with their rounded cheeks, bouffant hair, and rolls of belly fat, wondering if I lived in the wrong times. From Xi'an, we took another train to Chengdu. We got lost here too and frustrated but ate well. Full tummies make the inconveniences more bearable. We could not understand the language they spoke, which was a mix of Sichuanese and Mandarin. The sounds would come to us half or a fourth understood in our heads that we began guessing what they meant. At night, we went to what was the equivalent of an amusement park, but instead of characters from Western films or cartoons, it was an intellectual one celebrating Chinese art and literature. The park was festooned by red paper lanterns. At one booth, to keep things interesting, I made a wager. I told Medal I would send my future firstborn child to his Chinese school in Manila if he won the game where you guessed which Mandarin excerpt came from which book. I meant it as a joke because his school was notorious for keeping kids buried in homework and activities, never enjoying a moment's break. I knew he would accept it. The pages of the books were hung around us on a string like literary laundry; there were hundreds of passages. He gave his best try and did not win.

On the map, our journey began from easternmost China to the middle of the Middle Kingdom to its remotest region in the west crossing the country from one end to the other. The landscape did not change; the window kept me from the mountains, the snow. I experienced a bottled view as the window separated me, it also kept me alive.

It was free, uncensored and, even with our presence there, unconquerable. I wouldn't have survived out there on permafrost. Soil frozen solid for me was as alien a concept as seeing pandas in the wild, having lived in the sun and rain all my life. There was nothing more frightening to someone who was born in the tropics than the prospect of freezing to death. The snow looked like powdered sugar dusted on mountains highlighting crevices and creating shadows where there used to be none. Trees become even more beautiful with snow as if they were shaded in graphite. The reflection of a tired woman with a dishevelled head of hair stared back at me by the window. The journey was turning out to be more like a race than a vacation as we rushed to the train three minutes before it was scheduled to leave. In movies, you saw moving trains with the protagonist waving goodbye to those being left behind. The train was moving faster, gaining momentum when we jumped in.

The trip to Tibet from Chengdu took more than a day, the longest any of us have been on a train. We would sit in the cabin and stare at the window, which became a landscape television. The patterns of mountain, bridge, snow, mountain repeated itself on loop. As we traversed this sky road, we talked about our lives oblivious that we were on a journey in an area also known for earthquakes at high altitude. In ancient times, temples were built to worship the heavens and pray for good harvest with priests performing rituals that burned sacrifices to the moon and stars. Here we had nothing to offer the heavens but the sincerity of our intention to reach our destination.

Medal would unpack his Starbucks mug collection from the places we visited on the way here: Xi'an and Chengdu, laying them out like trophies on his bed. He collected souvenirs like he received awards — relentlessly as a competitive sport and a sign of value.

I made a silent prayer that he would never ever find a Starbucks Lhasa mug, or a part of me will be in tears. Prof. seemed more interested in Medal and shy around me, looking down at the floor sometimes or replying to questions with a non-answer. The hours were so long they dripped like thick honey, we ran out of things to say until there was silence and talk of the weather and the squeaky wheels of a depressing trolley cart which sold tea eggs and meat-topped rice meals. A sweet lady who went around with a cart tried to sell us packs of overpriced fruit. I walked up and down the carpeted corridor looking at the passengers, giving them woeful looks. I had experienced worse, like the rickety train we took to Hangzhou city standing up, hoping to rest for even a few moments on the wooden seats. The train was comfortable and spacious. It was clean like a plane because we paid for the hard sleeper beds. How did those who took the second-class seats fare? Our carriage had four berths with white sheets, a luggage rack, and a small table in the middle attached below the window. There were small lamps above each mattress and slots for you to listen to music or watch television. From above, the train tracks must look like a lasso of lines to tie an impregnable enormity. In a way, you could also say they were a form of unseen land sculpture only experienced in the way they dictated the ever-moving landscape you saw pass by.

After 24 hours of seeing the backdrop and another day to go, the view from the window became less and less appealing. We travelled all the way here to do nothing. The repetition became depressing, and the pleasure derived from it ebbed from watching the slow drip of ticking time towards a destination. The train began feeling like a prison, a tiny one in contrast to the wilderness outside it. The trip didn't seem to end, and waiting was like a pulled rubber band no one would let go of. We would journey the mountain range that pointed to Lhasa. There was a mixed sense of amazement and horror to know they drilled holes in those grand mountain ranges for tunnels to let the train pass through like stabbing holes in a wheel of cheese. I did not want to imagine how many animals were harmed, and villages moved to make way for the pass. The train was travelling at its highest peak at 16,640 feet above sea level while the rest of the track was at 13,123 feet above sea level. It would glide through a mountain, then darkness, then again, sunlight. I had never seen snow-covered mountains much less passed through it. My eyes were getting used to the view and the fantastic sights would seem less so.

This was us taking the longer, scenic route. We did not know what we were doing. The train tracks shaped a U passing by Xining, Golmud, Bodengguan, Nagque then Lhasa. Piercing through mountains as wide as cruise ships was part of the route. I was asleep when we passed through one again, but this time, instead of awe, I would feel like dying. I had miscalculated the time it would take to acclimate and woke up gasping for air. Everybody was fast asleep on their bunkers. I could feel the air being sucked away from my lungs; the air had become scarce. For a few seconds, I thought I would die. I quickly went down and put my head over the oxygen vents in our cabin. I lost more air worrying about a premature death than I ever did on the actual lack of oxygen. The air was thinner at higher altitudes as pressure dropped, making it harder to breathe. The night train on the way to Lhasa was a warning of what was to come.

We finally arrived after 45 hours on the train. The ground was pleasant to the feet. They say altitude makes the colour of the sky darker. We blinked and saw the bluer than blue sky. Tibet is often called the rooftop of the world because it was 11,995 feet above sea level. We alighted at the train station without anybody asking us for the travel permit required of foreigners. It was Tibetan New Year, a busy time. People were in a hurry. It was decided that taking a bus would be the fastest way to the bed and breakfast place we were staying at. On the way to town, Box tells me to do my part to ask for directions next time. He meant to do the part of translating; it was mostly Prof. and Medal talking for us while we tagged along. I shrugged off his comment, guessing he was projecting his language insecurities on me. I was not the one who had misread labels and taken one month to realize that his shampoo was really hair conditioner. When he asked me what was minority group in Mandarin called, his face fell when I said, *shaoshu minzu*. Box's grandparents were from Xiamen, who migrated to

Manila, and well, I wasn't ethnic Chinese. He was sent to Shanghai as a last-ditch effort to save the family legacy when his eldest brother could not speak to a Chinese trade officer despite three years in Beijing.

We were leeching off the fluency of Prof. and Medal. Prof. had photographic memory quickly recalling all the characters she studied since a child and Medal was a 23-year-old who spoke like a 60-year-old Chinese man because he knew the formal, bookish Mandarin coming from Taiwan. Locals understood him but giggled politely or scratched their heads when he used anachronistic terms. He knew the traditional characters of Hong Kong, Macau and Taiwan. In contrast, the mainland used the simplified version that it took him awhile to adjust his eyes to a world he knew in its complexity, not its abbreviations. The abridged versions had fewer strokes, a bare version of the original while replacing the meaning of traditional characters, still a controversial topic for many for what it means for cultural identity. Sometimes even Chinese teachers would forget how to write the characters midway having been used to typing it instead. Left on our own, Box and I would have been lost without them. I volunteered to handle the itinerary planning and booking the rooms through phone calls made at the back of the train so they wouldn't hear me struggle. I was embarrassed that they would listen to me talk.

In Lhasa, we ate Nepalese food and did not understand what we saw around us. There were beggars on the street in prayer. We moved to another place when the one I had booked came with an altar in the room which was typical of Tibetan households but creepy to the rest of us. The deities were unfathomable. The next day we went to Potala Palace along with a parade of pilgrims from all over on their way to pay respects during Tibetan New Year, the most important of their festivals. They were dressed finely in vibrant, colourful cloth or wrapped in silk scarves and coats with huge turquoise and amber jewellery set in silver like creatures crawling on their neck and fingers.

The temperature was winter cold but the light shone and shimmered like it was summer. Sunshine seemed to pour on everything around us compared to the dreary, darkened skies of Shanghai. The blue was the deepest in memory like a spilled bottle of ink. The colours refused to be ignored; the sun ablaze and proud. We walked around confused because we were following Beijing time. China spans five time zones but all must follow standard time, the capital. Our watches swung to official hours despite a sun that thought otherwise. It refused to follow set clocks; it was rising and setting on its own schedule. We did not listen, insisted on eating dinner when the light said mid-afternoon. We blinked at the brightness with regret: at the roof of the world none of us brought sunblock nor shades. The sun's light even entered my head, glared at every crevice, hidden thought and repressed image. After a day, Box and I began having severe headaches, shortness of breath and hearts that beat too fast as if caught in a race. A flight of stairs became a mountain to climb. Medal and Prof. were fine, which made us feel even worse, being the only two struck with altitude sickness.

The act of breathing had become belaboured. At the world's highest plateau, lungs struggled to keep me alive as did a lowland heart. We had travelled too fast, too soon from an altitude of 2,360 feet in Chengdu to Lhasa at 11,450 feet.

At the Potala Palace, climbing the stairs felt like carrying boulders up a steep incline. A white-haired, wrinkled woman beside me did it with no effort, like she was strolling in a park. I resented her for it. The Potala Palace was the holiest of holy places where rooms were filled with murals and line after line of people praying. And time. This was a place that had seen time unravel not in years but in centuries. It was as if their beliefs left a film that clung to the palace to make it a place of permanence. I imagined some of the Dalai Lama's things were still there when he left in a rush to flee at 23-years-old, never to come back. The yak butter candles melted in drippings of formed layers beneath them like hardened lava. The smell — gamey and cloying — attacked the nose as I became dizzy from the warmth, the people, the multiplicity of objects to see and remember and it seemed the rooms never stopped spinning.

*

The headaches and palpitations worsened as the hours wore on. I took on the sights with the throbbing lens of pain. The landscape became shiny, sunny hell. My head was leaden with shapeless thoughts, even food lost its appeal. Meals were yak meat with yak taste and yak scent — yak, yak, yak — that clung to you like a like needy lover. By night fall,

Box and I were united in our agony. I was not particularly religious but that night, I prayed to the God I knew and the other gods that could be out there: Buddha and deities of the Potala Palace; anyone that could make the acute throbbing stop, as if my heart wanted to leap off the chest. Box, bless him, told me we should go down to find medicine. We went around and asked, and since we didn't know the Mandarin word for altitude sickness — it was *gaofan* — we asked for what we needed by acting out the symptoms: I swayed like a drunk zombie and Box pointed an imaginary gun to his head. The medicine came in a carton box with test tubes filled with red liquid. We could not read the characters on the label but desperate people are prone to ignore caution. I took one and waited until Box opened his, we had become a team. With both tubes raised we toasted: To altitude sickness! To not dying, please! Box and I stopped annoying each other for being the weakest link in the group because we both were. Not only were our companions better Mandarin speakers, they felt normal, felt well.

*

The day before we left, we had run out of places to go. Tibet was the tail-end of a three-week trip on the road. We were wary of travel, of each other, of listening, of translation, and of complaining yet careful not to whine too much because didn't we want to be here? The comfort of routine was missing but more importantly we were running out of money. The next leg of our trip would mean another round of long hours stuck in a train back to Sichuan province then Shanghai. This time, we would not travel to Shanghai by that route, when we arrived in Chengdu city, the line to buy the train tickets after a holiday was as a local would tell us:

*duo de duo*
*tai duo la*
*duo de shobuliao*

These were new terms added to my vocabulary to mean that there were many, no hundreds, no thousands of people. The man guessed it would take us three days to line up to buy tickets.

But we would not know that yet, as we stood in the centre of Lhasa town by the bus stop on that very last day, no idea of what to do or where to go. Nobody brought a map; we were experiencing sightseeing fatigue. We were sick of markers of place; disgruntled of asking people where we were and how to find our way. Medal said, let's just take a bus. Everybody shrugged. We took the first bus that stopped in front of us without even asking where it was headed. It felt good not to care about destinations and let go of things. The bus drove around Lhasa, a city we barely even began to comprehend, to the centre of town again until it headed to the mountains outside the limits.

We gave each other looks: where are we going? The bus stopped beyond the borders where we followed people alighting and heading for a temple on a hill. The wooden temple was filled with Tibetans, or were there Chinese as well?

I could not tell for sure. There was no chanting or colourful fabric prayer flags. In the middle of the temple courtyard was a man tied to a huge post. The place was crowded with people staring at him. The post was so wide that he could not touch his hands together, bound as he was with thick rope; there were two of them. Isn't it strange the first impulse when you find yourself in a situation like this is to take a photo? That I should want to document this scene instead of living it because I did not want to rely on memory. A camera out in a crowd like this would be too risky; there was no choice but to remember. The last *chengyu* Kevin taught me was: *li suo dang ran* or according to reason, it should be the case. A man arrived with a whip to stand in front of the crowd then the men tied to the post; words were said before the shouts and lashings began.

# SEOUL

# Seoul Sisters

What I knew of friendships, I learned from my dead mother who made time to keep in touch with hers. I saw her friend crying outside the church in a corner after the wake. Blue would see me dabbing her face with a hanky before giving me a wan smile then nod. Mom, one of her best friends, was dead now, gone ahead and here was the daughter who was a twin in looks yet was not her. She died of cancer, a long and protracted march, giving both enough time to accept the inevitable. Close to the end, Mom stopped receiving visitors, more so friends, knowing they would cry more than she ever would as her face sank inwards each day. They were afraid for her, the cancer and even more terrified for themselves as if by another's impending death it was possible that they were the next in line.

I bumped into them at parties, supermarkets and said hi in the ensuing years, though seeing me made their eyes misty. Invitations continued to arrive in the house for the big events in their lives as if Mom were still alive to receive them.

Perhaps it made them feel better to see the family name on the list, to pretend she was present even by proxy. They had more memories of Mom than I did, a string of recollections tied together from being screaming college students at an all-girls school to meeting boyfriends to moving to a new city to start married life. I was not friends with my mother. She was the bad cop to father's good cop, the loving disciplinarian. A yellowed vinyl record found among the detritus of youth spent in a sleepy town in Bulacan would have the inscription: To Susan on her eighteenth birthday and with it a postcard photo of a woman in a dress with poufy sleeves. She would die thirty-one years later.

As I got older, I would nod when these friends talked to me about their lives, their faces stricken as if remembering another time with their long-gone friend. I would see Blue at wakes and there I would try to cheer her up, ask about kids. Town gossip spread, she was an abused wife, beaten and threatened by butcher knife and pocket pistol. Neighbours looked away because she married a known troublemaker, a bully. Growing up, I would see Mom with Blue go shopping, and share meals that stretched until late. I wondered then what she could have done if she were here. Would she have helped pack a suitcase when finally a bullet grazed her friend's foot? Would Blue have stayed in my room as she figured out how to move on?

A study by University of Kansas professor Jeffrey Hall says it takes more than two hundred hours to turn someone into a close friend. The hours tick faster for some people even if on paper you shouldn't get along having nothing in common that was measurable. You go on tentative friendship dates to see if you can enjoy each other's company, it could be coffee, lunch or dinner and wonder if the conversation will lead to anything interesting. There are people who become part of your life and share their stories that it feels like their peaks and valleys are yours too because of the many times it is repeated like a skit. One friend who hated having pictures taken only seemed to look good in photos snapped by someone she knew well and not a stranger. The smile was genuine, reaching the eyes while the body relaxed, knowing she was in good company. Maybe friends are the people you trust to hand a camera to knowing they would frame you in good light despite the double chin, the soft fleshy parts, the unflattering angles so the camera lens shows what they see.

It was past the two hundred-hour mark when Cheese and I decided to take a trip to Seoul, South Korea, where I would take dozens of photos. She celebrated birthdays as reasons to go to new places. It was our first time in the country having been curious to go because of K-dramas — *hallyu* — which led to the bigger slide to interests in Korean food, movie, music, fashion, design. When I told Korean friends I listened to a popular pop star, they would roll their eyes, sigh and shake their heads. I had mentioned someone not cool, even considered cheesy, and did not know any better because I was a foreigner.

We were on a plane flying in Korean airspace when Cheese turned 28-years-old. The camera I brought then was a Casio pocket, one the size of a deck of cards; the

first I bought with my own money and not shared with
the rest of the family. The camera was mine. I treated it
like an extension to seeing. Those were the years I took
photos of everything, every little thing that occupied
precious pixels and gigabytes space for high-resolution
images of pedestrian objects, of patterns on cracked dried
earth or parking lots filled with nondescript cars taken with
commitment like a documentary, of empty spaces or public
places not claimed by anyone but me. The past self made
it easier for these places to be written. So it was no surprise
that upon landing, despite being late and eyes groggy with
sleep, the first photo I would take was a lighted signboard
welcoming us to Seoul along with a photo of each of us:
one of me fourteen pounds lighter and her of fourteen
pounds heavier. The reverse would be true after a few years
on another trip. She encouraged me to take more pictures.
Her capacity for manic energy reminded me of an ad for
long-lasting car batteries, yet we got along well because
of curiosity and openness for new things and our shared
interest in getting the best deals. I was an introvert hanging
on the coattails of an extrovert.

We were giddy in anticipation and plans — what
we would buy, where we would go, what would we eat.
The excitement was encouraged by the fact that the
Korean *won* was down by half compared to the Chinese
*renminbi*, making costs cheaper. It was a sale! What luck.
We congratulated ourselves for great timing. The visa
counter officer did not share our enthusiasm and became
cross with me after watching me yawn while going

through my passport saying something in Korean while looking angry. This was lost in translation. In the Korean language, even rice is uttered with an honorific. What seemed like a harmless gesture to me was disrespectful to the visa officer, to look bored and tired while he was there stuck in his immigration seat with the clear authority over us. We were two unaccompanied women going to Seoul not joining a group tour. How could we navigate on our own? Independent travellers, more so women, especially women from so-called third-world countries, are a cause for suspicion. Could it be he thought we would work there or break the law because why would we travel alone and make ourselves vulnerable to misfortune? Male friends on knowing a woman who travelled alone would give a wink expecting they did and wanted what they wanted too: to collect flags from flings from every nationality when the more urgent thing that women wanted when they travelled was to be safe from men and not be killed in the process.

News of a woman maimed or abused while travelling alone is not unheard of though one doesn't need to travel for a woman to feel helpless, sometimes it happens even when at home. The immigration officer got grouchier when he could not reply to us in English. We presumed he was asking us where we would stay in Seoul and we showed the hotel address which was in English letters, not *Hangul*. His voice rose as he muttered more words in Korean with eyes glaring. Would he not let us enter the country? Would we make it here only to be turned away by early morning? Thankfully, another immigration officer took pity on us.

We were moved to the next lane to someone who was able to read and speak in English and was promptly waved away towards the exit gates.

We boarded an empty airport bus for the city. I continued to take bad photos aimed at indistinguishable objects because it was blurry or too dark. Cheese was too tired to notice or care. The hotel was a Hawaiian-themed one with tiki torches and pineapple prints in neon near the megapolis shopping area, Convention and Exhibition Centre or COEX. It reminded me that tropical fruits did not grow here because a Korean friend would ask if there were coconut and mango trees in our backyard. I answered yes, surprised at myself for taking the trees for granted while they looked impressed. I might as well have said I grew gold back home. The room had the usual amenities and, surprisingly, a computer desktop with not only free internet access but in speeds that swelled and gushed out of a channel like a river. There was no need to go through the internet with a proxy server because no websites were blocked or censored. It was the fastest internet speeds in the world. We felt like children led from a dense forest to a clearing with open sky where we could look up things, unencumbered. No information was blocked. We did not speak Korean, though, and knew the language would make it hard to get around in this age before translation apps on your mobile phones were available. Walking around the city meant bringing index cards with written questions scribbled in haphazard *Hangul* whose characters were written from left to right and differed from those of

Mandarin in their ways of referring to meaning because of their use of an alphabet. It would be easier to ask questions using those and less threatening than to let them figure out what we were saying. The only Korean phrases I knew taught by well-meaning yet mischievous Korean friends in Shanghai were: hello, love and motherfucker. On the cards were written: Hello! Could you please help look for ____? Sorry we are lost. We made sure to ask the first good-looking South Korean man we saw on the street for directions. He understood the *Hangul* sentences on the index cards and answered in English better than ours which made him even more handsome. Cheese's Korean colleague, Champagne, picked us up from the hotel and brought us to Doota Fashion Mall, a complex of retail shops that were open until five in the morning. Champagne loved to shop and suggested an itinerary without asking us. Cheese and I looked at each other. We were too polite to tell her we weren't interested in shopping, just food, but was curious what a mall that kept ungodly hours would look like.

Doota was in Dongdaemoon Market, a fast-fashion mecca and an environmental activist's nightmare. We drifted from one store to another, up and down the towers bathed in bright lights and white. It was a wasteland of things you didn't need. Salespeople were perky even at those hours trailing behind us asking best price, best buy in Mandarin and other Asian languages they knew. The energy of being there was wearing off, it felt like being hauled out of a loud party and thrust into daylight. Sleepiness melted many things into one lumpy mass. A family arrived with their children wide awake in tow to buy shoes at two in the morning. What started out as a novelty on the way there became a penance as we kept walking around at 3 a.m. in shops empty of people but full things to desire. Poor Champagne, worried that we were not having a good time because we ended up buying nothing. She would not get the hint right away that we were not shopping people by bringing us again to another outlet store.

The jubilation over the depressed Korean won was short-lived because no money exchange stall would open during the Labour Day weekend. The cash machines were also closed for the national holiday. We had a small amount converted at the airport expecting better rates in the city. We would be stuck with *renminbi* in our pockets unable to use them. There was money yet there might as well have been none.

Regret, oh regret when we realized it had not been a good idea to spend *won* for a *jjimjilbang* like the ones featured in television shows. The neighbourhood *jjimjilbang* suggested by Champagne had a *mokyoktang*, a female-only area inside the bathhouse. We planned to stay for half a day if not an entire one to make the expense worth it but wanted to leave as soon as we stowed our bags in the lockers. Everyone inside the *jjimjilbang* was nude. Cheese's eyes grew large when a middle-aged woman headed toward us naked and sopping wet with one hand holding a dry towel while water dripped down from sagging breasts to pubic hair to dimpled thighs to thick legs to form a trail behind her as she stopped by the stairs to stand. That was the future auntie version of myself right there, to become a no-more-fucks-to-give *ajumma*. I felt out of place, prissy and old-fashioned wearing a *jjimjil* uniform of a t-shirt, boxer shorts and the remembered modesty drilled in the brain and still unlearned from Catholic schoolgirl days. This disappointed me because I fancied myself a bohemian. How come they didn't show this on K-drama, Cheese whispered as we laughed at ourselves and walked further inside the bathhouse. There were women scrubbing each other's backs beside a pool. More half-naked women were eating bowls of ramen in a dining area while chatting. Do you expect me to scrub your back? I told Cheese. We both paused and said no at the same time.

There was a floor for rooms fitted with clay kiln ovens for sauna where no one was naked. The women looked peaceful napping with folded towels covering their eyes. As we lay there, legs and hands outstretched on the floor, I began sweating profusely. It was a 200-degree Celsius heated room. The floor was uncomfortable, the heat was spicy on the skin like Sichuan peppercorns. Fish on a frying pan must feel like this. Or menopause. Was this a preview of menopause? I looked around me and tried to hold on, seeing that they were calm, telling myself this was considered healthy, even therapeutic, but the more I tried to reason, the more I thought this was warmer than even the hottest of summer days in Manila. It would be a relief to faint. I wanted to faint but could not because I was lying down. What to do, what to do. No water. Time was baking us, making us regret the last of the *wons* paid for a sauna simulation of hell.

I imagined the immigration officer was laughing at us too knowing we wouldn't be able to take care of ourselves. See, what did I tell you, huh? In travel brochures, no one ever says that along with the sights and sounds of a foreign landscape or the other ways to live a life is that journeys make you realize how far from invincible you are. Not youth, not money, not even the most well-planned itineraries or intentions can prevent blunders or unfortunate timing. From feeling like we had more than we ever hoped for because of a soft exchange, the mood changed to beggarly. There was no choice but to make do with the dwindling *won* we still had. Champagne, who had business out of town, would be back in Seoul after a couple of days. We did not want to bother her. No one else could help us. Each *won* spent was counted carefully as if accounting for it would make it slower to spend and disappear from our hands. We wandered around Seoul, staring at food and letting our mouths water. The deprivation had heightened the senses. Cheese had become more energetic and positive assuring me not to worry though I knew she knew better than me. The money would last a few more meals and trips on the subway. Two days seemed long.

Kawaii was everywhere. Shops festooned with plants and pastel welcomed the teen girl's dream. I played with an adorable teddy-bear keychain, the stuffed toy attached to the chain was bigger than an apple. We held objects in our hands at the Insadong art street knowing we had to return it. Cuteness was a communicable disease here. There was so much cuteness, it was an end to itself for what did it matter that hair ribbons were in adorable checkers or polka dots. Despite the threat of penury, Cheese and I would blow our lunch budget on gelato and bowl of delicious cold noodles. In a building which seemed to have no walls or maybe it did but it felt like being outdoors while indoors, there was a courtyard in the middle of the four-floor retail area where you could bask in the sunlight.

This was our first trip together. It is tricky to travel with friends when you risk being exposed to your less than ideal self when tired, cranky or lost. Travelling shows sides of you never known, so does it show facets of a relationship that would never have been revealed in friendships spent over coffee chats, movies and restaurants. The anxiety of being in a new place makes you change routines. It was easy to let the small things bother you. The Hawaiian but not Hawaiian hotel near COEX replenished our mini refrigerator in the room each day. Since we were low on cash and shy to assert our preferences, we negotiated for the spoils of the mini fridge indirectly by way of who would be the first to wake up in the morning to get their hands on them. If you've lived with a friend and ended up not hating each other at the end of the day then she is worth keeping. There are friendships that only survive within the confines of controlled, separated spaces that don't involve leaving dirty plates on the sink or burning dinner. There were people who made perfect flatmates but you would have no business being friends with. By then Cheese was both one of my closest friends and flatmate.

If Cheese were the only friend I met in China, I would still consider myself a lucky girl. She would remain a close friend despite leaving the country and working around Asia. I went ahead then she a few years later to another country for work, I was afraid our friendship would not last. What if the version of myself she liked to hang out with, the Shanghai Joyce was not as fun as the Manila Joyce with her calendar now busy with family obligations and all manners of errands you had to do when you lived at home? What if her Malaysia Cheese was not someone I would like to be friends with anymore? This did not happen and we were able to stay friends despite the time and distance. Maybe it was because she was not demanding of your time and made the commitment to stay in touch. We would email each other important life updates or plan vacations together. I teased her that she had a friend for every country in the world. She was loyal, brave and supportive yet with her own sense of right telling me to save an extra helping of stuffed eggplant when another friend had yet to arrive. When I told a friend of plans to leave China for good to go back to the Philippines, she told me she was jealous. She envied me for the possibility of another new life: the chance to start over again. You can be another person, she said adding that you didn't even need to see the same people or keep in touch. Friends contribute to your happiness as much as they can turn it into misery. While most friends you met while you were younger with plenty of time to burn, fade away but you still keep fond memories of, there are some who won't give you the dignity of a painless exit. They think since you've been so loyal for so long that you will continue being there despite abuse heaped on you. Cheese was not like that.

People always talked about heartbreaks yet it is friendship break-ups that are in many ways more painful and traumatic than parting ways with a lover. Love stories are a dime a dozen, but nobody ever talks about good friends that stop being a part of your life. Nothing hurts more than being shut out by a person you trusted like a sister only for that to change and your presence barely tolerated later on. Friendship requires a chemistry of personality, common interests, generosity, a lot of laughter and the availability of time. No formal contract binds you to a friend but the pleasure of their company, not assets, not blood, nor obligation. They are there for you in the truest sense of the word and when you need it to knock sense into you. The sadness is longer and deeper when a friend you've loved for decades rejects the friendship like losing a keeper of your stories. Like any relationship, friendship also wanes and some branches will need to be pruned as one grows older. It is not wasted pain to stop being friends with someone after a few years more so if there were many good memories to recall. In botany, plants are labelled deciduous or evergreen for those who lose or keep their foliage. Some people shed friends like deciduous plants, dropping leaves at maturity depending on the season and stage in their lives when the companionship is no longer needed. For plants like these, this typically occurs in winter as a means of survival, of liberation and conserving energy to grow. For people it is no different when they are going through a difficult period in their lives while other people like to hold on to friends like evergreen plants choosing to nurture what they have rather than start from scratch. Friendships were not ties of nature and you were free to choose to continue or not.

So it was based on the foundation of this friendship that Cheese and I found ourselves roaming Myeongdong shopping street late at night, dejected and waiting for the cash machines to open. A man was standing in the middle of the road speaking with a microphone and carrying a placard with the words: Lord Jesus Heaven, No Jesus Hell. It was not farfetched to guess he was preaching about religion in a materialistic world. I pointed to the Samsung branding we kept seeing during the trip. There were Samsung cars, Samsung taxis, Samsung fashion, Samsung appliances. *Chaebol*, Cheese said when I asked, referring to huge companies controlled by families. We walked on and pressed our faces on shop windows imagining we had bought what was our heart's desire. Or we closed our eyes and imagined the taste of the food displayed under glass. I did not see Samsung food but wouldn't have been surprised by that too. A Samsung waffle would look like a microchip laced in veins of caramel, flattened and crispy like stroop waffle as an accessory to a complete Samsung product dream existence where the picture on the box was exactly what you got in real life. Every included part fit together and made sense.

Several hours would pass before the banks would open, until then I suggested coffee at the shop across. We still had enough money for coffee. Over there, I said. Look at that shop with red bricks. We crossed and realized too late that we were in the middle of a labour rally that was turning violent. Behind us were placards being hoisted up and down. A crowd of angry men were shouting. The chants stopped as they had begun; people started running, throwing bricks at the police. Would they use tear gas? What if one of us had tripped and been trampled on by the fleeing crowd? Where would we meet if we lost each other? Looking back, those were the times I travelled, feeling carefree, not thinking any harm would befall us armed with our plans, our maps, our hopes, our index cards of thoughtful questions when life was suffering no matter how much you planned it well, how no one gets out of it alive — it was the bingo prize everybody won. The rally was happening in front of the coffee shop. No one found it strange that there were two women in the middle of them. We just needed to make it across to be safe from these men who wanted blood and violence, their hands heavy with bricks. I held Cheese's arm praying that we would not be separated while we sliced through the crowd towards the well-lit, cosy place. No one glanced our way. We stepped inside the cafe where we watched the rally progress but with a benign interest as we regained our bearings, smiling at each other that we were at least unhurt, that we had escaped the chaos of what was outside in this safe place. People continued to sip their coffee and chat with friends.

Here was our same-moment bunker before we had to go out again in the big, bad world, where no man could beat up your friend just because he can. This time, I did not take a photo. We bought our own cups and watched as people outside ran and bricks flew in the air.

# HONG KONG

# Perilous Landings

NEW TERRITORIES: He shared a two-room flat with a banker from the mainland. 'So I can practise my Cantonese,' Five said but in truth, it was because living on an editor's salary, he could not afford downtown where landlords cut spaces thinly like bread with people sandwiched in between. He said, in this island territory, real estate was not a right but attainable only for the monied and of the monied. Sometimes he said the most obvious things. Wealth dripped through the system from the corporations to its bankers, stockbrokers working until late at night for the days, months and years it takes to afford an acceptable life. Someone would tell me that it would take him forty-two years to buy a flat to live in using his own salary. It was the same money built on the labour of Filipino and Indonesian domestics who would let those who worked for cash have the luxury to work for more. Five would see them go out for dinner, get drinks on a Friday then go back to work. They were the people he wrote about, talked to and hung out with that I wondered if he wanted their life of expense accounts, loyalty points, and business-class travel; and not in New Territories, living with a flatmate, wishing for money on islands claimed by foreigners.

I had flown to Hong Kong via a circuitous route: a Canton landing, a bus to the border, a wait at the train station, and a ferry to Lamma Island. It was our third month together having met at a Halloween party at The Shelter, a bomb hideout-turned-gay nightclub in Shanghai. I was dressed as a witch drinking a cocktail inside a gold birdcage, and he was a clergyman on a swing festooned with flowers. Witches and clergy have a lot in common; they can even know the same people. Emails and calls followed after that and he would come to Shanghai on assignment or I would go to Hong Kong during holidays and weekends. At the pier, I stood in front of a lady chanting in Cantonese, or was it prayers I heard, or both? She was kneeling on a blanket sprinkled with coins. Plastic-covered placards magnified mutilated bodies with the words, *Falun Gong*, a spiritual practice whose followers were persecuted in the mainland. Their organs were scooped out from their bodies like de-seeded watermelons. Five tugged at my arm to go, the ferry was here — boarding time. We held hands from Aberdeen; there was no way to the island but to cross water. Hands still clutching we arrived at sunset. There were no cars on the street, but there was space for trees now dappled with fading light. We walked to his flat, passing the shops and wet markets planning the rest of the days together. Later, while settled on his couch — an arm around my shoulders — facing an open window to a view of heaven empty of skyscrapers, he showed me a photo of the island taken from above. There was a semblance of a poufy head and a body with four legs walking up the islands above it. I said it looked like a disfigured poodle.

CENTRAL: I was in Hong Kong again for a fair of lights. Floors of light shimmered for every imaginable need and every conceivable form. There were globular lights suspended by wire and caged in shells of wire, wood and plastic. One thousand ways to contain brightness churned out by the factory of the world. I was there as an English translator for a Korean booth making solar power panels. A friend had recommended me to her father to help sell. I said yes right away knowing I would get paid for it plus get a free trip. Five would also be in town, and we would be able to see each other. Long-distance love affairs survived on small hopes. The fair was a business meet and greet for *guanxi* or networking, attended by; it seemed, the whole world. A man from Casablanca was pleased to know I knew his country. An Israeli businessman smiled at me saying his factory employed Filipino workers and his children were taken care of by kind Filipino nannies. I didn't know what to say, only to smile in reply. In my head, I thought they shouldn't have been there in the first place so far away from their family taking care of other people's children while their own are orphaned back home. The workers he depended on were probably yearning for the language and the food of home and spent nights messaging and calling

family and, if given a choice, wouldn't have left. He meant
no malice when he said it though and had an affectionate
look on his face like he knew me because he had worked
with so many of my countrymen. For the whole week,
visitors told me how they remembered the kindness of a
Filipino nurse or how they loved Filipino bands or worked
with Filipinos at sea. Why was it that I never knew what to
say after thank you?

I met Five at a Japanese restaurant where we had
been invited to dinner. The waitress was Filipina, and she
greeted me right away as she set the table and took our
orders. She asked me in Tagalog if I liked my work, if the
Korean boss I worked for was good to me and where was
I from? She had been working in Hong Kong for twenty-
five years, with no money saved and nowhere to go. The
story spilled out of her quickly from worry. I am tired, she
said, as her eyes became glossy. When will you go home?
she asked, I want to go back. The Koreans were amused I
was talking to a compatriot while Five kept his head down.
He pretended not to hear us chat, looking down on his plate
as if he saw nothing. What was he thinking? I sometimes
never knew. It was the same expression he had when we
passed by Filipinos on their Sunday break, squatting on
floors at an overpass or crowding parks with chatter and
trays of food. I would stare and smile because of the sight
of it: a revolutionary fiesta. They should crowd every nook
and cranny, stomp their feet, shout until ears ring, for the
work they do to keep this city running. This city would
gladly take their youth and labour but not give them the

right to stay no matter how long they lived there. Another Filipina was in the news that week, her back seared with a hot iron like steak. Five looked up now, his face was still blank. I tell her, I don't know when I am going home. I begin to say a lie repeated many times since then: It will be okay; you will be able to go home. We will all go home one day.

TSIM SHA TSUI: Wong Kar-Wai filmed here at Chungking Mansions pointing his camera to the maze and contours of shops never lonely for company. It remained as seedy as it was in the movie, *Chungking Express*, as if it were in a war-torn country instead of busy Nathan Road. I would watch the film again when I moved to China in the messy living room of our apartment. Five brought me here because he knew I loved the movie. We walked around retracing the imagined steps of the mysterious blond-wigged smuggler played by Bridgette Lin before she met the lovelorn cop of Takeshi Kaneshiro. They say this was where illegal migrants were brought and hidden among the sellers of counterfeit goods where cheap accommodations could be rented by the hour. No wonder it also earned the reputation for being a turf for mobsters. Why was it that in triad movies, half of their business seemed to happen over meals? I pictured the characters Lam Lok and Big D from the film, *The Election*, scoping their territory here while agreeing to meet for a bowl of noodles to decide the fate of the *Wo Shing Wo* gang. Or that Cheng Wing-yan played by Tony Leung from

*Infernal Affairs* standing in front a milk tea vendor — face tense with conflict from acting like a good cop pretending to be a criminal on the verge of a nervous breakdown. My eyes searched for the Wong Kar Wai colours that shifted, blurred and jumped from the screen. No French New Wave artiness here. There was none but drab. For that, there were other colours to see: a Pakistani diner in one of the many apartments upstairs where they say Hong Kong stars like Andy Lau would eat. Five was now writing food reviews for the papers and was eager to try it. He ordered the dishes labelled in English by pointing at the menu, by then we were too tired to try speaking in Mandarin or Cantonese. I stopped trying to speak the language in Harbour City when I saw the panicked faces of sales ladies who instead of trying to decipher what I wanted to say, shoved brochures in my hands. It was back to practising at neighbourhood shops for me. The diner was cramped, festooned by chintz, packed full of hungry people for a weekday night. We were the only Asians there, the rest came from parts of the world I would never know or visit. For the rest of the spicy meal, like them, we were also refugees.

YUEN PO STREET: They called it the Bird Market, Five told me, while taking photos for a walking-tour travel essay and jotting down interesting details. Well that's straightforward enough, I answer. We had walked from Goldfish Market on Tung Choi Street to see the shops lined with fish trapped in inflated bags of clear plastic heavy with water and air. They were hanging on the store front like banners or pinned to the walls like framed prizes. There were also turtles being sold with the fish because they were believed to cure cancer. He told me something else I didn't know. It was cheaper to throw out the fish at the end of the day than keep them longer. Worthless lives. I felt sad for the fish staring back at me, not knowing their future while I leaned to take a closer look. Goldfish in aquariums are kept for good luck yet here they are at the receiving end of bad luck. In Buddhism, it is good karma to release animals but what if they died in the process? The dark gutter may mean freedom of a murky kind. Or was it better to keep them trapped in plastic? These thoughts rattled in my head when I noticed a dog bend on his hind legs to poop behind a Tesla. Surely, someone else must have seen it too. How did a dog get to roam the streets of Hong Kong? Five called my attention again back to the Bird Market to see the man he had come here to write about: the oldest bird-cage maker on Yuen Po Street in his mid-60s. He was sitting quietly in his stall alone, hands still adept at bending bamboo to rounded angles and clamping them in tight and steady weaves. Five was careful not to make the man uncomfortable by sticking a tape recorder in his face. The stall was selling the bird cages stacked on the floor and on the table. No one will take after him, the art of weaving will be plucked and forgotten like feathers. The market was dying, even shrinking after the Avian Flu outbreak, and some shops have closed. Land was gold here and tempting to sell rather than continue with a business no matter how long storied or testament to culture it was.

Under an overpass, Five pointed to a rooftop where people lived in cage houses, bundled up for the winter months and sweltering in summer when vents would pipe out smoke and steam. He said he might write about them one day, these places he could not go to. After his notes, we headed to Border Street after stopping to rest at a playground with no children. We sat on a bench facing the monkey bars. It was his way of building up to a question: he planned to get a permanent residence visa soon. He asked me what my plans were if I wanted to follow him here to Hong Kong and take graduate studies. I didn't know what to say. He brought me to Border Street which looked like any street save that for four decades it was here that the British drew where Hong Kong began and the mainland ended. I looked above my line of sight thinking this was where people gambled life and limb for not just a better future with food, shelter and opportunity but a chance to turn your back on the past. I would have done the same.

LAN KWAI FONG: We passed by the marker of the most famous Overseas Filipino Worker who ever lived: National hero Jose Rizal on D' Aguilar Street and Stanley Street on the way uphill to a 24-hour diner Tsui Wah near the bars of Lan Kwai Fong. The 27-year-old Rizal had worked in this clinic as an eye doctor for eight months before leaving for Japan then travelling back to the Philippines to be jailed, then later on shot by the Spaniards. He would be renowned for his expertise even then. Would Rizal have partied in Lan Kwai Fong if he were alive today? He would die young at thirty-five years of age. It was in this city that their family would be briefly united under one roof. If I were Rizal's sister would I have minded being in the shadow of a brilliant brother who wrote and changed the world while I was left to clean the house and do the washing for hours? Would I have sold prized possessions and peddled on the street to support him in Europe? What if one of them had potential too, superior to even his? Surely, they wouldn't have spent time collecting girlfriends from around the world like him. I visualised that he walked this road coming from the steep steps from where they rented a flat at Rednaxela Terrace, a route he passed by every day, knowing he was being observed by a Spanish spy, Jose Sainz de Varanda, balding and bespectacled, tasked to observe his movements. Jose Rizal was not the first nor the last Filipino exile who would flee to Hong Kong to escape persecution. Hong Kong has been a site for revolution and subversion for Filipino patriots because they were free to plan. We were in the area for Tsui Wah for decent diner food. The restaurant had been a noisy and grimy prerequisite stop before and after a night of drinking for seventeen years in the area. Never go to the bathroom if you can help it. I ordered a plate of baked pork chops, a Macanese dish. Rizal must have liked Chinese food too. The exiled family hired a young Cantonese chef named Asing who cooked Chinese and Filipino favourites for them. In an interview, Asing would remember Rizal as a talented and hardworking doctor who never took naps.

Unlike Rizal, Five took naps liberally, so his ambitions of getting into a first-rate program for grad school was just that, an ambition that loomed larger than ability or reality. This would mark a phase in the relationship which began happily enough, as it veered slowly into an exile from myself. I believed in the delusions and silenced doubts as I helped him edit resumes and essays hoping that if we believed hard enough then it would happen. The anxiety was passed on to me and he questioned my own contentment because he had become unhappy in Hong Kong. A slow-burning career seemed miserable compared to friends who reaped the rewards of their high profile corporate careers. He was giving up on the writing which made me wonder if he planned on giving up on me too.

SHAM TSENG: The village made its name for having the best roast goose — it was the official mascot. We had lost our way. From the MTR, we rode the wrong bus and now had to retrace steps back to the part before the mistake was made. The right bus took us to what seemed the edge of a Hong Kong with lungs, a place of countryside and ocean blues. Five said we were looking for Chan Kee, a restaurant known for their fowl play, far from the reach of the tourist crowd. We praised ourselves into thinking that we were better than plebeian tourists for having found an authentic goose place frequented by locals. There were no foreigners here, I thought, as if it were a triumph. What fiction! Tourists have gone before us, how else would we learn about it? Five could have only known through a friend. At Chan Kee, the undressing of the bird came first. You walked past a man slicing an oil-shiny alluring roast goose on a wooden block like a bored plastic surgeon. He began by removing quivering fat from under the skin — my eyes watered at the sight of it — then carved the meat from the bones until it was naked. Locals like to eat roast goose without rice while picking bits from other dishes from a rotating lazy susan. Rice was considered a budget filler for those wanting to save money. Despite this, we could not help it and still ordered rice, not caring if we appeared unrefined to the other people in the dining room. The goose was sliced, fanned out on a plate like a carved mango cheek. The skin was luminous, melting on the mouth on contact. I could not tell if the goose was the best I've ever had; it was guaranteed to be better because of the effort we took getting there. It managed to meet expectations set by an imaginary standard of taste. As we shared the goose between the two of us, hungry bellies subsumed by hungry hearts, I wondered if the miles long journey to see him meant that like the goose, what we had was in fact very good.

QUEENSWAY: It seemed like the whole Hong Kong was there on a Sunday afternoon for high tea instead of their cramped flats. As a former British colony, Five said, it was fashionable. Sometimes he said the most obvious things. No seat was empty on this boutique hotel high up on a hill. High tea was all we could afford with our shallow pockets in this high place where a night's stay could cost a month's rent. Five avoided such places saying the prices made him nauseous, a hard thing to avoid on an island where even a good night's sleep had a price tag. Why not move to Shanghai then, I asked, the difference would not matter as much there. You don't need a lot of money to be happy, I said, which made me sound ingenious and a burden to a man crippled by status anxiety. It was the last day in Hong Kong for an umpteenth visit to the city. The relationship was waning; I felt burdened and judged by standards even he could not live up to. He was taking his MBA in Singapore, a sign of failure by his definition or rather by his friends. He was not good enough even for himself.

I drank the tea and spread the clotted cream on the scones, such pretty things on lace porcelain and a marble-topped table. The bite-sized cucumber sandwiches felt heavy in my hands as if we were actors in a play who had forgotten their lines. We strung the words kept hidden in spaces between arrivals and departures. The table beside us glanced our way, felt the mood change, the spotlight again shifted above us. His plans did not include me. I knew that for sure because he showed me the graph: a squiggly drawing of what he would do in the next years. He also drew a flowchart of whether we should stay together or not with options rigged to his advantage, of course. How thoughtful. It was the anxiety of making something out of yourself that was gnawing. He could not even find a job. What do you want, he asked turning the conversation away from him. I did not know what I wanted in life only that he should be in it. There were no fantasies of marriage or children that came to mind, I knew even back then instinctively that marriage was no dream but an excuse to eat well. The tea had begun to feel sickening, the cold elegance of the place oppressive. The sunlight that filled the cafe hurt the eyes. We had eaten a burger with fries before high tea as if knowing we had to keep our mouths distracted with chewing so that we would not say the things that needed answering. The food began to churn in my stomach; I looked at him wanting to vomit.

HKIA: For another generation who remembered another Hong Kong, to visit was to make a perilous landing. In the 1980s, the old Kai Tak airport was too short a runway, half jutting out on Victoria Harbour and half surrounded by high-rises. My mother would take this flight as a tourist while we would wait at home excited for the presents and stories she would bring back from travel. She would come back not with new clothes and shoes but with delicate pieces of jewellery for me like pear-shaped gold studs or a milky white jade bangle, gifts she knew I would never throw away. I would think of her back then riding that plane headed to Kai Tak. If the plane crashed on landing, the last memory of life would be of one looking out the window at the buildings that surrounded you as the plane made its descent: there the flickering lights from a television screen, laundry flapping in the wind to dry or the imagined table set for the next meal and the shadows of people behind them. Would they know you peeked at that one moment in their lives before your body was roasted like chicken? One could throw a ball from land and it would hit the plane. There is the temptation to wave a hello. A plane nearing Kai Tak skimmed over buildings, over people, like an overweight bird dragging its beak as it made its way past a checkerboard runway to make a sharp right turn. A life-affirming, heart-attack approach. Why was it that the most perilous landings were the most unforgettable? Because you survived to make an arrival. Kai Tak would close in 1998 to be replaced by Chek Lap Kok airport built on mountain flattened into a plateau. Pilots could no longer brag about their prowess when computers were around. Its roof was a geometric sky or the insides of a whale if its skin were delicate and transparent. Shops stretched for what seemed like miles and miles of never-ending gates. To be here was to be on the cusp of leaving for elsewhere. In my mind, I stood by the departing gate where I last saw him. Recollection says it happened in a moment from the departure gate to the plane to the seat to crying. I would keep the ticket of our last train ride together from Kowloon, rolling my eyes at the cliché of it all when I found it again and realized it was marked: single journey. The scene showed two angry people not looking at each other, in a rush to turn their backs to mask their eyes. I knew then that he would never speak to me again. I would see him at his favourite coffee shop in Central after, sitting across a woman who was frowning at his words. His back I could spot anywhere because it turned away from me at the airport. I didn't say hi this time as I passed behind him with friends. People hate those who leave them. I wished that memory was different but what is the use of proper endings? I wanted the goodbye that never happened when we could have looked into each other's eyes, known we had done what we could, smiled and lied: I promise to love you for ten thousand years like the emperors, for forever.

# MACAU

# At the Bay Gate

After I checked in, Maya looked at me with no other comment which I found puzzling, usually when meeting Filipinos overseas there would be at the very least the pleasantries of asking about where you come from and how long you would be staying. She manned the reception desk at the third floor of a bed and breakfast place in Macau, a group of converted apartments near the ruins of St. Paul's. I didn't take it personally and had other things to think about. It was my first time to travel abroad alone. I did not take the opportunity for granted knowing other women who wanted to do the same but was not allowed or did not have the means to do so. I was excited by the chance to go where I pleased, to follow my own plans and, strangely enough, not afraid though I should have been. Back then, unfortunate things had yet to happen and ignorance was a good reason for bravery.

The daunting task of travelling alone began with having no help with luggage. Going to the bathroom became a negotiation between your bladder or your bags. There was no second opinion to consider when deciding where to go to next. I had planned on staying in Macau for five days as it turned out two days too long. A former Portuguese colony, Macau was a smaller, sleepier island than Hong Kong and did not have as many sights to go around in outside the casinos.

They had no elevator. Coming from Shanghai on the way to Manila, my bags were bursting with things to take back and the load would not lighten even as the five days ended. Maya helped me with my luggage on the way up while heaving behind me asking why I had brought a heavy bag in the first place. She handed the keys to a three-bedroom flat. In one room was a newly arrived tourist like me while the remaining room was occupied by a middle-aged Korean man just waking up. I would later find out that it was his fourth month in Macau having left his family since to gamble day and night on the island. Maya would be friendlier the next day as I was ready to go out by inviting me to sit down for coffee in the dining room. She was from Mati in Davao, a beautiful seaside area many hours away from the city, on her fifth year working in Macau for inns and hotels.

Maya looked professional in her starched, ironed uniform with hair tied in place in a tight bun except for the swollen eyes. Her huge brown eyes looked like they were crying the whole morning or maybe the whole night. It was disconcerting yet she couldn't hide it by wearing shades. Ironically, you actually have more things to talk about when you meet a fellow countryman overseas than if you met them back home. There were the questions of where we were from, how did you get here, etcetera. We exchanged the basic questions, though I don't remember how the conversation shifted from talking about hometowns to talking about family. I realized that the silence and cold I felt from her yesterday was not annoyance but grief. She was a freshly minted widow with a husband buried last week. He was stabbed by a neighbour through the gut at a party the day before he was set to leave for Macau. They said it was a combination of alcohol mixed with small-town jealousy for having the chance at a better life. A job in a hotel was ready for him. Maya had waited months for him to arrive only to be told at the last hour that he would not come. She rushed back to their province to pay for his last trip to the cemetery. She needed to tell her story to someone who could listen. I sat there as if I was attending a wake and was not in Macau, one hand on a coffee mug and a bag lying on the table.

She paused, saying the kids were with her mother-in-law now. For her first paycheck, she bought her husband a music player and a mobile phone. This, she says, opening her palm to show a red iPod. They would earn more if they both worked in Macau, it would mean a comfortable life for the children, more help for people back home. They had paid a prohibitive placement fee to hire him and now she was stuck to foot the bill; an exploitative practice that buried you in heavy debt even before leaving the country. Abuse came from both sides, the Filipino recruiter and the foreign employer. I was able to avoid this because I applied to the job directly but this was not the norm. It could also have easily gone wrong for me with an abusive contract. The norm was a system that made it easy to fail and an exception to succeed. They called Overseas Filipino Workers heroes that prop up the economy with their foreign dollars but it was another way of calling sacrificial lambs without changing the system that compelled departure. Can you call someone a hero when the goal was survival not for glory or honour? Must the hero suffer in the end? She told me this in one breath, the frustration balled up inside the chest and leaking out of her face again. I kept quiet and nodded. There was the feeling of helplessness and guilt that all I could do was listen whenever I was told stories like these. Grief was another way to die. She would not be the last one to tell me their sad stories. Most came out of nowhere and without warning like sudden rain. The fact that I spoke the same language was enough reason to confess, that we didn't know each other didn't matter and even made them bolder to be honest, because they knew we would never see each other again. The coffee she placed in front of me was getting cold. I didn't know whether to hug her or pat her arm because she might start crying again. Fat tear stains scarred her blouse. I need to start cleaning, she said. Just as suddenly as she began her story, she stopped.

The next conversations I would have was in my head travelling the breadth and length of the peninsula from Cotai, Coloane until Taipa. They were once islands, now a peninsula separated from the mainland yet connected by cable bridges. I wandered the ruins of St. Paul, blending into the rest of the day-tripper crowd. Guidebooks tell tourists that the ruins are a must-do stop. People stand amid the rubble for the token souvenir photo and head to places laid waste by time and circumstance. Was it melancholy and nostalgia for a glorious past witnessed by none alive except these broken stones? Once one of the biggest churches in Asia, the facade of St. Paul is what is left after a typhoon destroyed the rest of it. One visits to see what is left from a life before. If the ruined were made complete again, was it still worth seeing? The St. Paul ruins is famous incomplete and damaged than it ever was in its heyday when it was whole. In Sweden, one of the main tourist attractions is a well-preserved fifteenth century ship which never sailed past the harbour. It was a failure when it could not fulfill its purpose but with the passing of centuries it became successful for surviving long enough to realize an unintended use. Maybe for some, the path to immortality was to let yourself go to seed like a gardening patch.

I relished the chance to follow or not follow an itinerary. I went into shops and flitted in and out as long and often as I wanted, not worried about what other people might think if I had companions to go with. I looked through stalls with their trinkets and delicacies without the urge to buy. I sat through a Portuguese Sunday mass. There were still expatriates who stayed on even after Portugal relinquished administration of the territory which once began as a trading settlement occupied by lease. I spoke no Portuguese but took to guessing what they were saying based on memories of attending masses. I took as many pictures of the inanest things without worrying someone else might get bored. A reflective surface, the outline of a lamp post against the night sky or a rack of egg tarts being sold at a shop front. I ate alone in a Macanese restaurant poring over the menu and decided a favourite order of baked porkchop rice and egg tarts despite originating here tasted better elsewhere. There was no one to report to or reason to be worried about not accommodating a companion's request or facing someone's frowned annoyance because they were not having a good time. I stared at a photo of an old Portuguese family at a shop that sold port wine wondering how they survived tumultuous history and changing hands. Did they decide to stay even after the Cultural Revolution? As a woman traveling alone, I tried to stay safe by not lingering in dodgy neighbourhoods or dimly lit places. I stuffed my face with sweets without care for calories or judgement for gluttony. Nobody thought it strange to see a woman by herself going around town but it felt like I had stumbled on a secret: I could see the world on my own. I could go to places without bending to someone else's wishes, without someone else in my head. If it rained, I could watch television instead and it would still be a good day. I remembered an aunt who was not allowed to travel by her husband alone or even with sisters. She was forbidden to have a life outside the family that even for exercise, her husband would accompany her — the ultimate oppression — you could not even sweat in peace. Her husband would scream at her like she was also a child that needed to be controlled. I always wondered if she was happy, if born in another time, would she still have made the same choices? One friend would tell me how she made her first trip alone at 42 years of age, leaving her husband and child behind, and was surprised by the freedom because it never occurred to her to wander. She rode the Disneyland attractions alone with no child or husband to care for and felt free.

There was a bus that took you from the centre of town to the south-eastern-most part of the peninsula to the A-Ma Temple. The oldest temple on the island, it is a place of honour for the sea goddess, Mazu, said to protect sailors and fisherman from typhoons. Similar to other cultures where goddesses protect shores, her blessing meant the assurance of security and home. Temple etiquette was unknown to me. I tried to be respectful and quiet. Mazu was a goddess and a martial arts fighter said to have duelled with other gods and won. Stone lions flanked the sides of the temple as you entered. There she sat at an altar in gold dress, her eyes closed, round serene face draped by a headdress surrounded by flowers and a tiled wall behind her. How did Mazu protect the island now a peninsula, Macau, when the Portuguese came four hundred years ago? This was where they landed, centuries ago, at the bay gate, looking for a trading port but deciding to stay longer. The temple remained the same while buildings grew in the landscape around it, dignified despite centuries of pirates, ship trade, world wars and the swarm of casinos that would come later on. When the last drop of squeezable dollar and profit leaves the island, Mazu will still be there. To her, you prayed for matters of death and life. I lit a joss stick for Maya, her husband, my mother and the others who have passed ahead. Brick red and spiral joss rings hung high from the ceilings unfurled as big as a waft of smoke like conical hats with no core that could burn for days as offering.

I did not see Maya again when I came back, nor the days after. Another would take her place who would not talk to me, only nod and say a greeting. The rest of the nights I walked around the island, wandering off to a park with a fountain where Filipinos gathered at the end of the day to chat and rest. They told me where I could buy a call card and the best rates for money exchange on the island. I was glad for their help even though they knew I was a tourist and wouldn't be around for long. It was kindness they gave that would never be repaid. I wondered myself that if I met them in the Philippines, would I have been as willing to help? I could go by my own company for three days and afterward would need to chat with strangers, anyone really, to hear the sound of my own voice. Taking the bus around the city was simple and affordable. I congratulated myself for seeing the island by travelling like a local instead of joining another tour group. The buses arrived on time, what took longer was how I adjusted to the traditional Mandarin characters instead of the simplified version from the mainland which took getting used to. The traditional Mandarin characters seemed to me more expressive, harder to write and entwined with meaning. Someone who grew up reading traditional characters told me they were beautiful. Macau was compact to navigate alone that I went through the sites in two days; out checking the checklist of the places worth seeing: the ruins, the outlying islands, the temples and the suburbs. The city had traces of its past as a sixteenth century Portuguese trading settlement. I had underestimated the efficiency of a solo traveller. On the remaining days, there were no other places to go to but the casinos.

What else was there? Macau was touted as the new gambling capital of the world to feed the mainland's pitless appetite. I walked along the boulevard lined with casinos, sat on a bench overlooking the quiet water reflecting back night lights. From the comfortable position of the bench, my stomach full, feet resting and eyes taking in the view, one could pretend that in Macau, there was more to life than money. This was not true, of course. The Wynn had opened with its hundreds of rooms and hundreds of tables for gambling. I snapped photos which looked bright and electric that it was hyperreal to be there; the fake lights prevented the real night. The casinos' bling and sparkle was dazzling but also alienating for me who had no gambler's itch to scratch nor would ever be excited by the possibility of losing hard-earned money on a whim.

It was not my first time to be around casinos and boom, bust cycles. The earliest memories I had of them were of the ones opened in Clark Air Base after the Americans left. Friends and relatives began working at casinos for higher pay. Card games at home were played with boxes of rejected Bee Club Special cards which were thicker and had the satisfying click when shuffled and cut. They were sliced on a corner and had a punched hole in the middle to prevent cheating and ensure it would never be used again. We began going to dinner at casinos, watched a show on a cramped stage of American women strutting in sequins and glitter before family and friends went around the crap tables trying their luck. People dressed for the night. It was a sign of the economic boom promised to Pampanga along with the renaming of the airport from politicians wanting your vote. But they were just words as jazz-pop singer Basia crooned: *Promises/We forget all our promises/ And only keep some of the easiest.* I went to the slot machines because they were the simple to understand: pull the lever and watch the pictures align to bingo. The enthusiasm of business after the Mt. Pinatubo explosion was premature and would die down. The Duty-Free malls would shutter and look like haunted houses. The money would leave again as abruptly as it had arrived.

I was worried I might not be able to go inside the Macau casinos because I was wearing slippers and shorts. I need not have hesitated because the gambling folk were dressed shabbier than I was in faded jeans and holey t-shirts. They were like me except I had no wads of bills on my hands sprouting like fists ready for a fight. There were free peanuts and drinks in trolleys for the players in these carpeted palaces of money. With a snack in hand, I stood beside a man who had a two-inch stack of bills framed in each hand as if he planned on using them to fan his face. He did not look wealthy — real rich people hardly do — was short and slim in a shiny polyester shirt, forgettable shoes and faded jeans. A cigar was sticking out of the side of his mouth while a bag full of more money lay on his feet for everyone to see. What was surprising was not the amount of cash but that no one had tried to steal it from him. The people around us were nonchalant about the sight of cash out in the open then I realized they were here not for those pieces of paper but the thrill of losing and multiplying wins and losses. I, on the other hand, by then, had just enough *patacas* to last me until departure.

As I stood there, I wondered if the man had earned his money illegally in the mainland before crossing over to Macau? Was he an official raiding government coffers? Or was he from Guangdong, a factory-owner's son who cinched a huge manufacturing deal? This was the only place in the country where betting was allowed and before online gambling would drive the vice to overseas shores and many years later reach even the Philippines in massive numbers. Macau was prepared to welcome the millions who would come to try their luck and lose it. He could have been a border criminal on the run, which makes the idea of seeing him there more exciting. Or a triad member cashing in which would explain why the money in the bag was of no concern. There was news about cross-border crimes coming from the mainland that ranged from human trafficking to underground banks to drugs. They said it was easier to commit crimes from the Special Administrative Region or SARs to the mainland than the other way around. Border crossings were made over water. To get to Hong Kong from Macau, I would have to take an hour-long ferry from Taipa. The other gamblers in the room were heavy with cash as much as their hands, bags and pockets could carry. It didn't matter what they looked like as long as there was no end to the roll of the dice. This was not Las Vegas where gambling came with the glamour and glitz of movies and music and tall tales of gangsters walking in plush surroundings.

I tried to fit in by snacking on the free food and finding a place to sit. No one paid me any mind. The gambling folk were in a dazed concentration like zombies. They did not look like they were having fun either with their faces focused intently on the hands being dealt. Games for money were games of memory, matching and recognition knowing when to show your hand based on incomplete information and gut feel. I spent the rest of the night watching the movement on the casino floor and pretending I knew what was happening with the cards. No wonder people looked tired; there was hardly any sleeping. My throat started to itch because of the smoke and the lights strained the eyes which began drooping, drooping as I almost fell over the seat. It was time to leave so I headed out weaving in and out of the tourists who came to the casinos like the faithful on a crusade with the hope for the miracle of a jackpot and the thrill of an answered prayer.

I would see Maya one last time before leaving as she helped me zip an overpacked suitcase and drag it down the stairs. All I could tell her was to take care and thank you for the hospitality. The Macanese *patacas* did not last until I left, but sooner. My wallet only had *renminbi*, and a few US notes to maybe buy a convenience-store sandwich. I was also worried that I would not have enough money to make it to the airport for the flight back which rolled into anxiety about not being able to afford the extra kilos. My attempts to use *renminbi* notes from the mainland at a shop were received in contempt. You are in Macau, the man told me shaking his head, we do not accept *renminbi*. I explained that I had run out of *patacas* adding that aren't we in China! Is Macau not China? As soon as I finished saying those words, I knew it was a mistake. The statement was met with, even more, what seemed to me like hurt pride and scorn. This was Macau not China which may be a part of China but was, as he corrected me, not the mainland. Macau was a Special Administrative Region allowed to have its own rules, language and money even though it was under Beijing. This was a blind spot because I was not Chinese, to forget anti-Beijing sentiment and how they wished to distance themselves from the crimes and horrors committed by the government. It seemed to me at that moment that they physically shared the same territory but socially it might as well have been a different place. I would read the same sentiment plastered on Taipei newspaper headlines adamant at maintaining their sovereignty. So there I was, corrected and hungry as punishment. I had to walk further until I found a money changer but had to beg for consideration when she said the notes were too creased to swap. There was more head shaking, the print on the money seemed faint she added, it could be a fake. I began pulling out the notes and smoothening them by hand, careful not to make the indentations on them more pronounced. I turned to flattening the paper bills with a book while also keeping feelings of panic thumped down in my stomach and not make it rise up to the throat. In the gambling capital of the world, I could not believe my currency was not money.

# ULAANBAATAR

# How to Ride a Train to Ulaanbaatar

## 1

The first step when riding a train to Ulaanbaatar, Mongolia, is to miss your flight. The check-in counter closed five minutes after she arrived. She thought the Beijing fast train was what it said it was but expediency turned out to be one and a half hours long. With mounting dread, she walked as quick as she could until her legs hurt but all seemed endless; the escalators kept getting longer; the hallways constant; one door led to another and another. The airport loomed like China: all-seeing and unmoved. Every traveller's worse fear is to get lost en route to a flight. Her stomach began to churn; lips puckered dry. She rushed to the Mongolia Airlines office to beg, cajole, and beg again in Mandarin, then in English, finally both. No more flights in the next three days, the stout woman who played the roles of check-in counter person, office and plane staff, told her. Midsummer was the time of the

Naadam Festival where people flocked to the capital to watch the traditional games. She adds, you will need to buy a new ticket. The woman shook her head and treated her as she was but denied until then: a girl who had been left behind. The ground was not the ground; the world was shifting sand. She staggered outside and began sobbing like a child. No one to help her. Knees buckled until she was on the floor, bawling. Fat tears quivered on her chin. This girl was ugly when she cried. The mouth was a down-turned smile and the full cheeks pockmarked by red from the effort. The janitor, disturbed by the sight of a woman uncontrollably crying alone, stopped to asked her what was wrong. Wrong? I planned this trip for four months, she thought. She stared at him through watery eyes. Of course, he couldn't understand. *Ni hui shuo Zhongwen ma?* he asked her if she spoke Mandarin. Four months of searching, calls and emails; of saving and imagination. Four months of waiting gone in five minutes. She had told everyone of her adventure — to the Land of Khan turned to a cannot. She cried for her stupidity; her loneliness; for being at the right place at the wrong time; for the familiar dread of being left behind yet again. She cried until the crying turned to grief; she cried for her mother.

## 2

The habit of crying in public began at the grocery store two years after graduation. I shoved three packs of adult diapers in the cart. Three packs for my mother; sick for months now.

The hospital bill was trapped in a conjuring spell writing itself exponentially in the language of the terminally ill. I had images of being the heroine in a bad telenovela selling cigarettes on the street. Who would be so kind, I wondered? Friends? Relatives? Money is like water in a cracked pot when you are so close to dying. I knew my father borrowed money. How long would that last? Dying would be cheaper than living. Drugstore managers knew me by face because I came often and bought the medicines they kept under lock and key. Doctors would drop by the room to chat and greet me in the hallways. Medical students on shifts wrote about her on their notebooks in terms of detachment: metastasize, carcinoma, distant spread, prognosis. I was roaming the hospital in tattered clothes or reading newspapers in the sitting area in slippers. I called the nurses by their nicknames. In the afternoons, I would tape my mother's voice using a recorder from a journalist to remember what memory might soon forget but it was too late by then. I never cried in front of family. Turning to friends for solace was moot because they would begin crying first. I ended up comforting them; tapping their shoulder and assuring them not to worry. They wished I wouldn't bring it up. But here in the blandness of the tissue aisle, I could cry as much as I wanted. I sobbed while walking to the snack section; wiping my tears as I decided between tortillas or potato chips then whimpered my way to the freezer for ice cream. Grocery shopping was therapeutic. Nobody looked at me or stopped to ask what was wrong. They were too busy with checklist lives for a stranger.

## 3

There was another way by land from Beijing. Take an overnight bus and a van; cross the border then ride the train to Ulaanbaatar. Three days, you could take a bunker, Tracy from the travel agency said. The next day the girl is on a bus on its way to Erenhot in Inner Mongolia. Instead of seats, beds were crammed and stacked from one end to another. A bag was tucked under her head as a pillow while another hand clutched her tote. The bus was full of Mongolians, mainlanders, and two other foreigners. Twelve hours on a bus in a July night-time journey alone. What was she thinking? There was no scenery, only blackness. A thin blanket covered her. She could barely sleep from the excitement for the plan hatched on the fly but fatigue was slowly taking over. It would be four more hours before they stopped for a break. A Mongolian woman with high cheekbones and unblemished skin looked curiously at her. Often the girl was mistaken for Chinese until she opened her mouth to talk. The awkward words and accent were the traitor — she learned her *putonghua* in Shanghai. It was without the sounds of the standard Beijing accent. The dim light and the steady rhythm of the bus became a lullaby. She felt her hand loosening its grip on the bag. She would get to Mongolia, she knew it. The assurance came from uncertainty. She remembered her mother's warnings of rape, harassment and violence from men. A woman travelling alone is perpetually neurotic but the thrill of escape overthrew fear. She couldn't keep awake. The lull of travel was a seductive call to sleep.

4

The year was 2008 at the Philippine Overseas Employment Administration in Ortigas Ave. when I registered to become an Overseas Filipino Worker (OFW). I was there because my mother died. If she were alive, my father liked to repeat, you wouldn't be allowed to travel alone, much more work in another country. We were ushered into a crowded room littered with school chairs and no air-conditioning; an old fan the semblance of comfort. The speaker was a lady in her 40s who spoke in a loud voice to explain the pre-departure seminar tackling salient topics such as:

How to Fill in Immigration Forms
How to Pack for Your Trip
How to Ride a Plane

No one is exempt from this, in the eyes of the government we were cattle to be herded out, out of the country. They don't want you to go but only half-heartedly because pockets are fuller if you do. Remember, she says making her voice louder, the airline food is free. Don't forget to eat so you won't faint. If you faint, they might send you back, she warned. She saw me looking bored and asked: Are you sure you want to leave? What if something happens to you? Do your parents know what you're doing? I answered, yes.

Leave it to the bureaucracy to make even death bloodless. An employer must sign a contract with the promise of action in the case of death for the hapless Filipino worker written as, 'repatriation of worker's remains and proper disposition thereof.' My mind wandered on what kind of box they would ship me back in if I died. A recycled fabric-wrapped box for China? A biscuit tin? Would they add oolong and jasmine tea to my ashes for scent like potpourri? By FedEx or the cheaper EMS? I hoped there would be no pain. The last time I saw my mother was in a box — a bronze one — before they sealed her in another made of pink marble. She was the second cadaver. The first one being my namesake, my grandmother, who I would chaperone as she was wheeled out of the room to the morgue in the bowels of St. Luke's Medical Center. The third would be my uncle, who would burn in an oven wearing his favourite suit; his arms flailing to the sides as if he was still alive but it was the spirit of the flames fighting to get out, not his. Ashes should be kept in one place, so I was told, unless you wanted him resurrecting with missing body parts. I pressed my eye to the hole to see this, the burning; the first of my cousins to do so while the others waited behind me. It was one relative's idea of educating the next generation about life. The fire was glorious, terrifying. He would have been pleased to be so thoroughly burned.

After a year in Shanghai finishing Mandarin lessons and an internship, I was hired as a business editor for a publishing house. A far cry from my first job when I was a public-relations writer tasked to attach blurbs to society photos while feigning interest in brassieres and stale sandwiches. The writing was to sell not for opinion. The work visa felt like a new contract for life. How do OFWs die? In many, many ways. Years ago, my mother died before fifty from colon cancer. If I am the fourth cadaver, I wouldn't mind an IKEA box finished with a polka-dot ribbon, but there was no form for that.

# 5

The journey paused past midnight on its stop halfway to Inner Mongolia. The girl stepped down into the cold to see nothing but woolly darkness — as far as she remembers. She could say, I also saw horses where we stopped since it was Inner Mongolia but that would be a stretch even by her imagination. Were they passing by Hohhot? She didn't know but it was the city she could name. What she knew for certain was there was a shed intended to be a toilet. Intentions are fragile things; they tend to miss the mark. The shed's link to a real one was a hole in the soft ground. There was squatting and balancing involved as she made sure her jeans would not touch soil; her left hand held the tote bag bulging fat from a camera while her right tried to stop her mouth from gagging from the stench. Years will pass and the image of that stop would blur and quicken on the truth of the horrors of that moment. There are times in life when you know, you are where you are meant to be. For the girl, it was taking a piss in the middle of nowhere; aiming for a hole overflowing with shit.

She did not die, just imagined she did. She cursed herself and the American who encouraged her to go here.

The Mongolian girl who stared at her spoke: Are you Chinese? They tried their best to talk — she spoke a little Mandarin. They made do with a motion of hands. Assumptions would have to be made. In her head, the girl thought of the lovely Mongolian as a scholar sent by the government to study Mandarin for trade. The Mongolian girl, on the other hand, imagined that the quiet Asian was Indonesian and not another mainlander in search of business in Ulaanbaatar. Both sipped tea in silence to keep them warm in the dark.

## 6

People always remember the first year away. I could still expect phone calls on my birthday. To this, a long-time China resident would tell me: Wait on the second, and the year after that and they will soon forget you. It was inevitable that as the years went on connections with friends and family in the Philippines started to fray. The friendship I offered was replaced by others; shared memories displaced by happier ones with someone else. My presence in Manila was a yearly marker, not a constant. I would go home for the occasional wedding and be there during Christmas holidays. With grandparents, mother and uncles long dead, the link that held me to the rest of the family tree unraveled. They knew my mother not me even though I looked like her. Squabbles among her siblings made the rift worse. Being away, it was easier to believe the illusion that the life I knew before remained unchanged.

I collected friends to make a version of family. How straightforward it was to talk to another foreigner and at once share something in common. To laugh and say: Look at this strange place, do you understand what's going on? No expectations existed beyond brief encounters. Secrets were kept safe and locked by anonymity. I can believe that you are the person you hope to be, while you can think the best or the worst of me. Always there is that one person who becomes your best friend during a flight, says Karla, a college classmate who moved to Dubai as a flight stewardess. Three years and it still thrilled her to sneak into the cockpit to watch the moon drift by. Kinship with other foreigners in China felt like moon watching in a way. The point was to look.

7

Borders tell of sketched portraits and winding fortunes. The girl was standing on Inner Mongolia, now part of China since 1947. They shifted boundaries but kept the name; like pocketing a jewel with the owner's label still inscribed. If naming was a form of possession, then in a way, Inner Mongolia was still part of Mongolia if only in bitter memory. The bus had stopped at the China border town of Erenhot. The maps were lying, this was not the mainland. It was a crisp day capped by a sky that hinted she was on the fringes of the place of destination — Ulaanbaatar.

Gone were the fog-choked clouds of Beijing and Shanghai; this was a sky for blue believers. She dragged her bags following the other foreigners in the bus — Michael, an Irish man, and Kai from Osaka. Travelling alone teaches you to be shameless, to ask for help, to be dependent even when the girl prided herself on the illusion of control. There was no choice but to have trust in strangers. She approached Michael just after they arrived in Erenhot asking if she could go with him on the journey to Ulaanbaatar. Michael was scrawny and tall with dirty blond hair and spoke with heavily accented English that she could not understand. He also looked like he had not touched water for a week. Kai, overhearing them, piped in if he could also come. He was no taller than the girl, dressed like he was on his way to a desk job instead of an adventure. Michael agreed and said he knew someone who could arrange for the rest of the trip. We would have to wait in that hotel, he said, pointing to a dusty building with its signage in disrepair. Two of the letters were gone and one was tipped to its side. Erenhot was a border town full of the sadness of stillborn dreams. The vision was a bustling place alive with trade; the reality was a hollow mall with frameless windows like gouged eyes. For Michael, Ulaanbaatar was a return to his Mongolian wife and son after Ireland; where he said people had lost their homes and livelihood to the mortgage crisis. Life led him to Mongolia for a vacation that turned into six years. I've lost faith, he said, we are doomed. She hoped what he said would not be a premonition, being where they were, a place to pass by and turn your back on, not to stay. Places like Erenhot became spaces for departures. Late lunch was noodles at a diner. Michael said, let me talk I speak Mongolian. Like the girl, the waitress could not understand what he was saying. The girl would order for them but this time in Mandarin.

## 8

What would you do for love? I asked myself while attending Mingming's baptism in a cathedral in Shanghai. He converted because he was with Maricel. The Chinese do not date, they marry. To marry her was to be Catholic or she would not have said yes otherwise. Mingming joined the church choir, attended classes and made Filipino friends. He professed love of Manila even the country. (Nothing flatters Filipinos more.) His English improved which was a boon for his marketing job for a German firm. He was the sole convert for that winter day as the priest poured water on his forehead. I have seen curious locals play with the water font at church, even taste it by licking their dipped fingers as if relishing something delicious. The cathedral was framed with the glow of dozens of candles. It was solemn, it was romantic, it was beautiful with the hum of the choir but most of all it was freezing cold because being a Catholic comes with no heater. There is always hell for that.

Months after, Maricel would get married to Mingming wearing a rented white lace dress in a seafood restaurant downtown. The place looked worn and dark-eyed as witness to hundreds and hundreds of lauriat-besotted celebrations. The lovely bride, a little bewildered but otherwise beaming, would enter the ballroom to the tune of *Marlboro Country*. Her mother fixed the wedding veil dragging on the floor. I touched my mother's pearls, pearls she bought while with her own mother. I wondered, who would stand in for those brides who are unmothered but not motherless? The host went through the motions of Western rituals with the wit of imitation. I heard the collective gasps from the conservative Manila titas when the cigar-giving and alcohol-swilling began in earnest. The mother in my head would have done the same. Mingming went around offering the best smoke and *baijiu* they could afford to male guests. Refusing was impolite. What the place lacked in looks it made up for taste — it was one of the best meals I've ever had in the mainland — which I enjoyed too much because a guest asked me if I was expecting child. Love does make the world go round.

9

She held the ticket to the Trans-Mongolian train on one hand and took a photo of it with another. There were too many photos of her life abroad as if she were chronicling it for someone other than herself. The ticket was in Cyrillic, a show of Russia's long history of alliance and influence in Mongolia. Some of the letters were in Latin or were inverted but for her, it might as well been scribbled inside a pre-historic cave or beamed from outer space. Her eyes hurt from blinking, she could understand the numbers indicating the time, presumably. They were heading off the beaten track by taking this part of the Trans-Siberian Railway, so off beaten, it's been open since the 1950s. Anxiety gripped her as she was worried she would again miss a scheduled departure. Was she even given the right ticket? There was no time to worry for long. She and Kai started taking photos: of the train, the carriages stripped of cargo, people sitting on their suitcases staring back at the vast nothing and the random spoils left by travellers. Click, click, click. The girl wondered if she would make it. Why this road in the first place? Her friends asked her the same question but here nobody wondered why that they were riding the same train heading for the capital needed no explanation. She could say she wanted to go because of work — reports written, researched and filed in the country for her job. Or she could say it was because of the stories told by friends and strangers who fed her images of riding horses in the Gobi and sleeping in a yurt. Batu, a classmate in Shanghai, told her of life in Ulaanbaatar where there was no fear of getting lost only of not moving. It was certainly not because of the horses because the girl played no sport and did not even climb trees.

Maybe it was for the lure of land crossings. From Erenhot, they were taken to the gleaming marble and pressed-uniform efficiency of the Chinese border office facing the Mongolian side to have their passports stamped. She imagined this was where borders were pushed and held back in 1919 when Chinese soldiers began invading

Mongolia to expand territory. They were gathered again to leave China in a van. Nearby was the Mongolian border control which had the casual air of a bachelor uncle's car garage. The floor was untiled; there was a line to a makeshift booth where a woman paused to look at her passport before making a call. Her heart raced, she had come this far to be denied again. Filipinos are allowed visa-free entry to Mongolia for twenty-one days unless the rules changed on her way there. If she was not allowed in, was there another way to go? No was a hard answer to accept at the border. These are the thoughts of a stalker, the girl told herself as she fidgeted and waited. The woman said, stand there and look up. She stepped forward on a mat to face a camera hanging from the ceiling. The mat read: WELCOME.

## 10

Parents will send their lucky children to live abroad with the ambition that their child will be less Filipino, less local, more cosmopolitan and talk about the world with the air of a weary sophisticate. The opposite also happens: you become more Filipino, more of yourself. You can't walk away from who you are any more than you can deny liking what you eat paired with a steaming plate of garlic rice. How else would you be able to delineate otherwise? When each encounter leads you to question what you believe in, then you will have no option but lay your claim. The specifics could be as trivial as preferring soda instead of wine or drinking cold water during winter. Wait long enough and as years abroad pass by there comes with it a remarking of your own land crossings. Nationality is a label for belonging but what if you decide to belong to no tribe but your own? The box of who you are could be bigger now. The failures and disappointments of age forced you to either enlarge or stunt yourself. Like cats, people loved their boxes though. Gemma led a comfortable life working as a highly paid English teacher for an international school in the Shanghai suburbs. She secretly hated children and even despised reading but was scared to leave because of the money. A chance to study in New Zealand was dropped because failure weighed as much as success. Misery was better than uncertainty. As for me, boxes are dark, cramped spaces. I like to poke holes with a switchblade. How will you let light in otherwise?

## 11

The girl pulled the striped curtains back. Today, she boarded the train headed for Ulaanbaatar. The conductor was a plump woman in uniform who asked for their tickets and passports. She looked through Michael's and Kai's but stopped to gape at the Filipino passport in her hand. Was it because the girl looked miserable in her photo or that she had never seen a Philippine passport in her life? The woman would pass it around the train before smiling and returning it back to the girl. She could not sleep now and it seemed, so did the other passengers. The moon perched on the Gobi like an owl. All were silent in adoration.

She sat on the bottom bunker of a four-bed carriage with Kai in the bunk above, Michael across her and a Mongolian woman taking the one above hers. A hand appeared, the woman was offering a pack of biscuits. From Shanghai, she said. She, like most people on the train, wore loose faded clothing as if the sun had followed them all their lives. My sons are studying in Korea, she would tell the girl. Michael woke up and sat cross-legged on his bed while Kai climbed down to sit on the small chair in the middle of the carriage. Tapping his pockets for coins, Kai began unburdening himself by giving away his spare *renminbi* to the girl while pointing to the red linen scarf on his neck. He planned to travel to Mongolia for five months alone. Lightness was crucial; there was no need for these things in the desert. Conversation with Kai was a dialogue with his notebook where questions were written and answered. He wrote, you want the scarf? The girl nodded her head. She wrote, wife? He smiled and showed her his wedding ring while removing it and tucking it into his shirt pocket. They went back to staring at the moon.

## 12

The world is less chaotic when you are looking at it through a box. The years in China were the closest I've been to living in a surveillance state. There were CCTV cameras everywhere. Each apartment transfer or hotel stay required a registry of passport and visa for scanning and filing. You must report your address to the nearest police station as soon as you arrive in the country each and every time. No matter how lost you were, the government always knew where you could be found. The ready phrase I used when I did not know where I was: *Duibuqi, wo milu le.* Be foolish enough to travel locally without a passport and you would be refused a place to stay. Follow the rules, stay inside. The internet groaned with effort because websites were filtered, skimmed and trimmed for controversy. Even a possibility of dissent brought it to a standstill. If you think about it, though, who needs constant surveillance when your mother is dead? The voice on the tape had become the voice inside my head. She is more powerful than any all-seeing eye even a Chinese-made one. In bathrooms, I cannot escape her judgment while showering, only ignore it. Sometimes.

I read the news with the eye of a jaded lover. Rumours say that even the sweltering summer temperatures were lower than actual. What else was tampered truth? Truth is malleable when you live away from your past. To some, it is a way of acceptance. Howie would feel most at ease with his private self in a country that abhorred the word. In Shanghai, he could wear purple fedoras, pearls and hand-painted shawls while hugged tightly by a French boyfriend. He could be himself and betray no one. His mother could keep the illusion of her eldest child locked inside her heart and ignore questions of his penchant for fans. For others, China meant freedom or a small measure of it. An Iranian friend would bring me to their New Year celebrations for music, booze and crazy dancing. Parties are illegal in Iran. So it was not dance like no one is watching but dance as if it were never forbidden. She was ten when they visited Tehran one last time, smuggling a vial of rose oil in her skirt before migrating to the United States. The fragrance of crushed rose petals reminded her of home. She would ask me: Why are you here? I would say with my head dizzy with vodka: for adventure, of course! It wasn't far from the truth. China was then the great turnaround story; a country changing so fast the world couldn't keep up. It was conflicted and brought on conflicting feelings of equal parts admiration and dismay. I thought that if I was around so much change, maybe I could change with it.

## 13

Leaving is never as memorable as arriving. To finally say after that long journey: I am here, it is over. When you arrive, the time of departure becomes reality. This was not home. You are not meant to stay. The train passed two mountains shaped like a sleeping woman's breasts and the girl knew the hours of waiting would be over soon. She could walk on real ground, not this moving platform. Nothing would ruin her mood. Not even the Filipinos she would bump into at the grocery store. They were there for jobs and tried hard to contain their curiosity by asking: What was she doing here alone? In this far off place? No, no. There were hills near the city and she could peek inside a yurt. She would remember a photo of two boys taken in a field of such boundless space that she envied them for their privilege. She would eat yak meat and yak butter and regret her tummy ache after. Russian caviar, vodka and chocolates were sold at convenience shops. She would marvel at the perfect sky on the day of her arrival: unfolding joy. Michael would smile at her when she asked for his email knowing that they would never see each other again. Kai would say goodbye to join a group of teenagers in a rented jeep. The girl was excited nevertheless, she had made it. She was in Ulaanbaatar.

# 14

Two years would pass before I would come back to Shanghai in 2013 after leaving for good. A day was spent on a pilgrimage of my old life. This was where I bought my favourite dumplings. On this street, my bike was stolen twice. I remember missing the bus stop here but I would find the right trail back. These stops were meant to make sense of a catalogue of souvenirs. Everything smelled the same; the trees were as gnarled as ever. The city was framed for my viewing pleasure. I gazed up from a bench on People's Square Park at the building I used to work in. From my desk then, I could see the spot where I was sitting now. The Moroccan-styled bar by the pond still served Happy Hour cocktails. This was the park for the Sunday Marriage Market where eager parents posted leaflets and resumes in their quest to find a suitable partner for their beloved only child for a type of love that could be found by the alignment of one measurable trait to another. I was happy living here; I can't imagine going back. I often wonder where that girl

went, the girl who went to China alone knowing no word
of Mandarin to start a new life. Would my mother have
approved of her? Was she still here? I don't recognize her
in photos. Scientists say memories were never meant for
nostalgia but survival; the last step. My vision began to
blur. Eleven years after her death, I stopped crying for my
mother and began crying for myself.